CHIPS ON THE FLOOR

Dad and Mum with 'Joey' — 1919

CHIPS ON THE FLOOR

The Memoirs of a Very Ordinary Fellow

Jos J. Smith

A Square One Publication

First Published in 1992 by
Square One Publications, Saga House
Sansome Place, Worcester WR1 1UA

© Josiah J. Smith

British Library Cataloguing in Publication Data.
A catalogue record for this book is available from
the British Library.

ISBN 1 872017 61 4

Typeset by Avon Dataset Ltd., Waterloo Road, Bidford-on-Avon B50 4JH
Printed by Antony Rowe, Chippenham

Acknowledgements are due to my wife, Edith, for her patience with my tappings on the typewriter and with thanks for all her help in so many things over our 42 years of happy marriage.

My thanks also to Yvonne, for her very professional work on my manuscript . . .

PREFACE

Statesmen, Generals, Politicians and famous people write memoirs in their retirement. Why then should not a very ordinary fellow do the same? This work might interest a few folk who may also be very ordinary, but in any case the writer is enjoying the recapture of many incidents and folk who did so much to provide a full life.

What we are at any one time is the result of influence. The end product of environment, example set by others, our search for identity, all play a part in producing us.

Read on then if you wish, and share the joy of being alive and well.

FOREWORD
by Richard Baker, O.B.E.

I don't want to accuse my old friend Jos Smith of false modesty, but the fact is that the author of this volume is very far from being an ordinary Ordinary Fellow. I've known him for years, or thought I did, but I wasn't aware that he'd constructed a road through the Syrian desert with little more fuss than he made about building his own bungalow. I was only vaguely aware that he'd done that, though I suppose the name of his house 'Weedidit' should have made it obvious.

I first met Jos when I was presenting the South East Regional TV programme 'Town and Around' for the BBC. We were doing a report on the David Livingstone Club for Handicapped Young People at the then new town of Harlow in Essex, and I was impressed from the first. Jos did me the honour of asking me to be President of the club, thus revealing another of his talents, that of arch-persuader. He's not a person it's easy to say "no" to. But who'd want to refuse? Here was a most remarkable creation, a Club uniting people with various forms of disability run by people who, like Jos, would consider themselves ordinary but were altogether exceptional in the quality of friendship they offered to those less fortunate than themselves.

The David Livingstone Club, which started as a small gleam in Jos Smith's visionary eye, has grown and developed in the most remarkable way with the cooperation of the Shaftesbury Society. It is a model of what can be achieved by single-minded devotion and determination. It is all the outcome of a profound religious faith which was guided Jos all his life. For the former Sapper it's been a case of 'Onward, Christian soldier', and I'm sure you will find his story, told very much in his own style of talking, full of inspiration as well as common — though not ordinary — humanity.

Richard Baker

Chapter 1

World War I saw the birth of many famous people, so at least the writer started with level pegging — on the thesis that all are born in the same way. For all of us the first few hours of life are similar. Feeding, being washed and changed, not forgetting the patting on the back to remove wind. But how soon things begin to change.

At Dover, my town of birth, life for my mother was very difficult; it was equally hard for many other mothers too. Father was away soldiering in the Middle East, and the only adult male that I knew was the Sergeant billeted on us. I will never forget how cross he was when at the tender age of two I pushed his cane into the fire. Years later I knew the meaning of some of the things he called me. (Truly, I am sure he didn't mean them).

I was three when my mother prepared me for father's homecoming, and I began to think that this wonderful person had won the war single-handed, chasing Turks away into the desert. Eventually he came home and brought all kinds of interesting things, such as little elephants carved from ebony, clay pipes and paper knives made from spent bullets. I thought that he must have been a wonderful soldier to have all these things when all the Sergeant had was a cane which I had put into the fire. In those days I never realised that in twenty-three years I would also be a soldier serving in the same area as my father. He was demobilised in 1919, and as the years passed I learnt the art of being one of a family. There was Dad, Mum and me — I liked it.

For many families life in the immediate post-war days was a struggle, and not quite the state which "heroes" had hoped for. It puzzled me why my dad had to go out at seven in the morning whilst other dads stayed at home. My dad came home very tired, and other dads (although staying at home) looked fed up. My father did at least have a job. He was a grocer, and soon became the firm's representative. Believe me, his round of calls on shops for orders necessitated his covering up to forty miles every day on a heavy old bicycle! The company car was a luxury that had not reached the deep South of England.

Summer and winter my father pedalled his way around the South Coast collecting orders from little shops which all played their part in the building of a better Britain. When he returned after his long day he was certainly not able to put his feet up and rest, as there was all the day's takings to tot up and record, ready for the firm in the morning. So skilled did my father become at totting up figures, he could add up three columns of figures at once. His copperplate style of writing and neatness in presentation of his sales reports were exceptional. He left school at the age of twelve!!

Yes, life did have its difficulties, but there were standards unknown today. There were loyalties and commitments to duty that mark a great nation. Much of those days we never want to see again, but (and the writer does not wish to be too prophetic) — we will, unless people forsake the God "Gimme".

At five years of age my mother took me to St Martin's Infants School in Markland Road, Dover. On the second day there I found my own way to school, as I began to realise that in this big world you have to stand on your own feet or be pushed aside by some "smarty". This is still the situation in life, except that "smarty" has grown up and has a different name.

St Martin's School was quite small and had a strong affinity to the Parish Church of the same name. The Vicar seemed to us small children to be the most important person in the world. He came to the school quite

SOUVENIR

OF

PEACE CELEBRATION TEA

GIVEN TO

Children of Lascelles Road, Dover,

BY

Parents and Friends, 25th July, 1919.

= God Save the King. =

Joseph Smith

3

frequently, and from my infant observation it seemed that if you could say the 23rd Psalm the Vicar assured your entry into Heaven. The Psalm was for the small children, and the Apostles Creed seemed to be the passport for the older boys. He did his best to direct us in the Anglican tradition but never seemed very thrilled that the Methodists along the road had a good football team. The writer owes much to the Church of St Martin. Without this early training he may never have been a Free Church Minister. We travel the same route and our many differences can Unite rather than Divide. The Parish Youth Club and Brass Band (activities which were in being long before the State took them over) gave us the foundations of a tradition of which many old boys are justly proud.

Every year all the young people of the Church would march three miles for their annual Sunday School treat to the Elms Vale conker pond. It was during the brass band years that I had been relegated from cornet to side drum for playing "Bye-Bye Blackbird" one afternoon in our front room at home. This sort of music must not be played on the church cornet. We set off on the outing from the church, and as I had the drum it was my job to lead the column of young people to the conker pond. After stepping it out for about one mile I thought that the rest of the band was playing rather quietly — in fact I could hardly hear them as I rounded the corner by the farm. Looking back quickly, I saw to my amazement that the band was not in sight. My long steps brought my career in "brass" to an early end. Once we reached the conker pond field we played the rich man's game, cricket. Really, it was the Vicar's opportunity of showing his skill at the game. We did get a knock later on — one over each and the Vicar was bowler. Need I say that I was out twice in one over? With the game over and the stumps pulled, the Vicar directed us to a large elm tree, where he said grace before we consumed large plates of hufkins and muffins. We always enjoyed the outings, although the one described saw my last efforts with the band. When it was all over we marched back — three miles.

Many of us in those days owed so much to Captain Stevens of the Church Army. Because he wore a uniform and a big hat he was to us far more important than the Vicar. On reflection, he was more in touch with us young folk as he knew life at our level. To raise money for the purchase of table tennis balls at a penny each, the Captain organised us into a minstrel troop long before the Black and White Minstrels appeared at the Victoria Palace. Never was "Jingle Bells" sung with such enthusiasm — encouraged by the knowledge that after the show we would be able to enter the local table tennis league. In those days there was no Youth Service grant available from the local authority, and everything that was done was the result of our own efforts. But so much of it was made possible by the Captain. If the writer had to name someone who was responsible for "pointing the way" then it would be one who never made his pathway into the halls of fame — Captain Stevens of the Church Army (1927 – 29).

During my years at St Martin's I was still at school. The Church and school ran parallel. Our headmaster, Johnnie Hunt (as he was secretly called by the boys), ruled with strictness and never was his authority questioned. I remember how he dealt with the problem of boys smoking in the "dubs" area. They were invited by Johnnie to be present at his study at four o'clock one Friday afternoon. He called them in and bade them sit down. He then passed around some very large cigars and they all lit up — not much choice really. By ten minutes past four there was an enormous cloud of thick smoke coming through the joints of the door, and five minutes afterwards a group of very sick boys emerged. Few of them, if any, ever smoked again. Mr C Weeds was a senior teacher at the school who did so much to help those of us who had failed the scholarship examination which gave entry to the Dover Grammar School for Boys. He taught us how to "get by" in French, the elements of geometrical drawing, and how to use a log table. Our drawing office consisted of pieces of plywood cut to fit the basin in the "dubs". The reader will by now appreciate what the "dubs" was. There were few jobs about and no handouts, so we knew that Charles our teacher was working for us. I never remember any boy letting him down when he put us on our honour to work without supervision. If one had he would have been well and truly thumped — by the other boys. Of course, schools were different in those days; the school meant something to us, and it does today fifty three years later. At the Old Boys Dinner each year when the toast "The School" is given, one or two still have a lump in the throat as we think about those days with the "Saints" and remember the lads who did not return in 1918 and 1946. At the dinner there are still one or two very elderly "boys" who were there in 1918. Few schools can claim such devotion from those who attended just an ordinary elementary school, and few can claim the successes in achievement by their lads.

It was during the Twenties that there was real hardship in the land. Dover had little to offer in work for adults and even less for school leavers. The writer recalls the days of the local soup kitchen. In a class of forty there were only about six boys whose parents had jobs. The six took it in turn to walk to the soup kitchen carrying a large clean galvanised dustbin and a sack. Generally the team consisted of three boys, and once they had reached the kitchen the bin was used to hold as much soup as the boys could carry. Two boys boyhandled the bin and the third carried the bread. The journey back to the school, a distance of nearly two miles, was arduous, but what a good lesson it was. Some of the boys had no boots or shoes. Slippers were not very good in the middle of winter, and it was Miss Baker who from time to time managed miraculously to produce footgear for those who needed it. Oh yes, there is hardship in 1981, but there are many today who so often quote the word when they just don't know the meaning. Let's not spend too much time on looking back. It happened and it's behind us. Mrs Eaves and Miss Baker, the school's lady teachers, were indeed saints of the highest order. For as many years as they were able to be present at the Old Boys Dinner they were given a place of honour at the top table. One year at the Dover Town Hall, I believe it was in 1962, we were all seated and awaiting the speeches from the selected members. Captain Kingsland began his speech, which to many of us seemed a little long after ten minutes, when a firm female voice was heard to say, "KINGSLAND, sit down!!" Like a lamb he resumed his seat, and amid the laughter which followed he said that in that moment he had gone right back to his classroom days when often Miss Baker dealt similarly with his enthusiasm for talking in the classroom.

After the Second World War the Old Boys Association arranged for the reinscribing on the honours board the names of boys who did not return in 1946. The builder carefully eased the marble slab away from the wall, and — surprise! — they discovered the cane of the first headmaster of St Martin's embedded in the mortar. The cane was later presented to the reigning HM with great ceremony. Tradition? The school has affection for its pupils and its pupils loved the place, which for them has no equal. One thing I did notice on my last visit: the playground which once was sloping had been levelled. What a pity! It was such fun sliding down the slope when there was ice about. However, the writer doesn't really mean this — it's much safer being level. Bricks and mortar can be changed but the things that matter are unchangeable.

At thirteen I attended Confirmation classes which the Vicar held in the vestry. He explained many things to us, some problems were with his wisdom solved, but others I found more perplexing than before. He gallantly tried to put us right; told us that God cared about everyone equally, but when I asked why it was that so many men did not have jobs, especially when they had served their country so well during the war, he gave me the most helpful reply, "Some things you have to think out for yourself." The Confirmation service was presided over by the Bishop of Dover in St Mary's Church. It was a big event and the church was full. Perhaps, I thought, it was to square up their non-attendance on lesser days with the Bishop and the Almighty. I saw neighbours at the Confirmation who possibly went to St Martin's only on Easter Sunday, when they had a new hat. Oh yes, and most of them were at church when someone in the family was married. It was all very puzzling to a thirteen year old boy, and it still puzzles me at sixty five. Please, dear reader, don't think that here is another cynic laying the pathway for a tirade against the church and all forms of authority, because I firmly believe in the law of the land and our obligation to respect it.

The Bishop in his address to the candidates for Confirmation made a particular point of stressing that we had reached the age of discretion, although here again I am still wondering if one can pinpoint an age when this condition comes upon us. When the Bishop said this it made up my mind for me. The following week I joined in the Methodist Fellowship for worship and became a Freechurchman. I am now a Congregational Minister and owe my allegiance to the wonderful folk in the Parish Church who showed me that the Christian way of life was one to follow. Of course, the tradition of worship pattern was different in the Wesley Hall Church, Chapel, Hall or whatever you care to name it. The essential point of all places is that within the shell of bricks and mortar we all meet to worship God with other folk who seek so to do. I remember entering a mosque in Damascus to worship

God, and the Temple in Jerusalem for the same purpose. Some readers may be a little shocked at this, but did not Jesus enter the Temple to worship, and another time chat to a Samarian woman of doubtful reputation beside a well? The Great Temple of our Creator is not restricted by architectural whim, building regulations, economics or the nodding approval of an ageing Committee member. Where you are God is. So watch it when you are tempted. Even that Northern Ireland parson when he parades his "army" should remember that in the eyes of the Creator he is no better than a starving infant in Africa. However, this work is not intended to become a drawn-out sermon, so we will move on.

Schooldays were rapidly drawing to a close, which would leave one with the difficult task of finding a job. My main interest was to make things out of wood, mainly because wood was cheap, easily obtained, and if I wanted plywood my father produced a tea chest for 2d (old money). Strange, is it not, that when we had the old money everything seemed so much cheaper. I did not know the difference in those days between a carpenter, a joiner, a wheelwright or a fencer. A fencer to me was a sort of latter-day knight complete with horse. So long as it was working in wood I didn't mind what the label might be.

The next chapter begins the story of employment which influenced my life. I must never forget that basically I am a wood worker — a carpenter. And if the reader thinks that this is an odd background for a Congregational Parson, then just reflect for a moment; God's Son was a carpenter in a village called Nazareth and His workshop was not very big. There's nothing cheap about a craftsman, and believe me the world's many problems will be on the way to being solved when there are far more people able to DO something and far less telling others how it should be done.

I was fourteen on the 20 May 1929, rearing to plunge

into the workaday world and put all its mistakes right. I knew most of the answers, and industry should have been pleased at my entry into it. WHAT SHOCKS I WAS DUE TO RECEIVE! Anyway, now — as the "grace" says — I am truly grateful. This is the end of this chapter, so for the reader it's an ideal time to break off for a "cuppa".

Chapter 2

This chapter begins the "Chips on the Floor" in a very real sense. It is the episode in which the writer entered the building trade as an apprentice to the trade of carpenter and joiner. The undertaking side of the business came as a bit of a surprise during the first week at work.

Near to my home was a small builder by the name of Jesse Morgan. Jesse was a Baptist Lay Preacher and Deacon of his church. He wore a fascinating cap which was in sections, having a little button on top. I thought it looked like a little crown of glory. He had a beard, rather big; and to me he looked like an Apostle 'cause all the stained glass windows I had seen presented the Apostles with similar beards. Jesse engaged in speculative building — Council contract work and occasional undertaking. They didn't call them morticians then, unless you lived near London and paid a lot more for the same service and, without doubt, the same end. My mother and I visited Mr Morgan in July to find out what the possibilities of employment were for a boy who wanted to work in wood. Jesse offered me a job at 2d per hour. I was to work for him for five years, serve with diligence and loyalty and be prepared to help out in other trades if there was not much to do in actual woodwork. Great! I had a job and the prospect of earning money.

With a new apron, pencil and two foot rule, I went to work on Monday of the following week. As soon as Jesse had handed me over to the foreman, Bill Wood, and then made his way back to his office (the glass extension to his house), Bill took one look at me, found a broom, tossed it in my direction and said, "Here boy — take this and see that there are no CHIPS ON THE FLOOR".

At the end of the first day, feeling rather tired, I was told to "Get off home and come in early the next day as we have a box to make." Bill also said that he would measure it up on the way home. It was all a mystery to me because I couldn't see anything to get excited about in making a box. Anyway, the following day might reveal all — it did!

Arriving at the workshop early, Bill (I always called him Mr Wood when he was in sight) came puffing into the yard like an old steam engine. "Bring up some elm wood — wide ones — 1 inch thick. I've measured him up and it's got to go home today." By then I realised what it was all about. We were going to make a coffin — on my second day at work. For hours we planed, scraped and sandpapered; poured in hot pitch, button-polished the visible surfaces and put on solid brass handles, and made sure that the lid screws had a little fat on the threads. It puzzled me why the screws were fatted. I asked Bill and his reply was "So that the old gent can get out easier. You should know all about that — you go to church, don't you?" said Bill. It took years before I knew what he meant.

At half past five it was all complete, so I took off my apron to go home. "Where do you think you are going?" said Bill. "Home", I replied. Bill came back with "Not ..... likely! You're coming with us to box him up. Dash home, put your best suit on and come back in thirty minutes looking holy". Back in the time limit, looking smart if not holy, we loaded the box on to the handcart, covered it with purple velvet and made our way to the home of the deceased. As Bill met the widow and very reverently asked if we were too early, he became a different person. Gentle, almost holy looking as he talked to the lady, he reminded me of the Bishop at my Confirmation. Once we had the box inside, Bill reverted to being Bill again. "Put up the trestles and stand the lid to one side till we get 'im in." Once the deceased was in,

Bill made his final check to see that everything was in order, and then told me to stand to one side whilst he brought the relatives in. Bill showed such pride in his work, he looked to me like an Archbishop. My first box on my second day at work at the tender age of fourteen! I know on reflection how good that coffin looked, and I had my share of work in it. The Boy began to grow up quickly. We provided these last services about once a month, and in time I thought nothing of it; it was another job of woodworking. Today, as a parson, I look back over the years and think, when I conduct a funeral, "I've seen this at both ends of the event." The mortician and the officiating minister have a duty to honour. Both are concerned to serve the departed with dignity and respect, be they Lord or Pauper.

By the end of the first week I had truly earned my 8/4d old money (42 pence in today's money) and I had a job — as an apprentice.

It is after the first week at work that one has a chance to size up the job, to start to know one's workmates, to know where the various storerooms are, and, most important of all, to settle down to the period of training. Tools for the trade were very expensive in relation to an apprentice's 2d an hour. It was in this connection that my mother came to the rescue. She had a bright idea. Why not make fireguards from odd scraps of oak strip and she would make fabric panels to fit? The cost of the finished article in those days was about 1/6d (or 7p). They sold to friends for around 4/- or 20p. Over the years one was able to collect a large number of tools, and indeed I am still collecting them. I notice in the trade journals that my old tools are now worth twice as much as the original cost.

I was assigned to work with Bert Newman for the first year. Bert was a very skilled craftsman who during the war had worked on fitting of some of the flying machines. He taught me to ask every time I marked out any material which had to be cut — "Think twice and cut once." Bert also taught me that a "glory box" into which went all kinds of oddments would save pounds in years to come. During the winter months there was little work about, and to keep us employed Jesse Morgan put us on making ladders and wheelbarrows. If you want to learn how to saw straight, just find a fir pole 20 feet long and rip it down the middle using a hand saw. The ladder rungs were of oak or ash, if we could find any in the store. Many "clever" townies think that the country craftsman is "C" stream grade in matters of skill. Dear reader, don't believe this. The countryman is the backbone of the national heritage in many skills. To make a wheel in wood by hand calls for the highest skill, and the pride you have when you see for the first time that your wheel turns without a wobble! Today, of course, people have to buy these galvanised iron "barrers" which last five and twenty minutes. Days have indeed changed. It's progress, or so they tell me. Bert was of this old skill, and I shall always remember when together we made about thirty wattle fence sections — you know, those delightful fences which grace the fields in Kent and give protection for the sheep and make the meadows look real countryside.

Every Monday morning Bert brought a clean apron to work, and at the end of the week it was nearly as clean as on Monday. You should have seen mine! "Mucky Pup" was his favourite retort, and it took many years to get anywhere near to his standard. In fact, I never have.

We made more coffins in the winter when there was little other work on the houses. People buy their homes in the spring and summer, and die mainly in the winter. Every November we could expect Bill the foreman to charge into work one morning and tell us that his old aunt was kicking it (this means failing and likely to die). He seemed quite disappointed when she rallied. He had reserved for her a set of oak boards. To quote Bill "There's nothing like a good bit of oak to give you a big send off." Each coffin had on the lid a brass plate for the

14

name of the deceased person. The writer in his second year was given the honour of writing the name. It meant two hours overtime and sixpence. You could do a lot with sixpence in those days; 3d to get into the pictures, a cup of tea and a sausage roll — then walk home.

Our firm had no lorries, and Jesse Morgan had only his "bike" to do his rounds. Many of the men said that was a good thing as they could see him coming. Needless to say, those in the firm who didn't pull their weight were soon rumbled and sent on their way. Jesse built up a staff of craftsmen and labourers who set standards often unknown today. How many of them come to the mind of the writer, there was: Bill Holbrook — the Signwriter, Fred Bliss — the Painter, Jack Hogg — the Bricky Foreman, Harold Pelham — a Joiner, Len Manning and Jack Bulman — both senior apprentices and nearly out of their time when the writer joined the firm. The whole process of learning the trade was one of passing on knowledge. If you had good mates then you were lucky. We had no part-time day release classes at the Technical College, so if you wished to pursue the finer points of the technology of the industry you made your own arrangements with the Evening Institute or School of Art.

I was greatly encouraged to study the trade by Harry Hedgecock. Harry was a craftsman of exceptional ability. He taught me how to sharpen a saw by standing behind me holding a little piece of lath and "correcting" me if I lost the right slope of the file. He taught me in 1932 and now in 1981 I'll sharpen a saw quicker than anyone — all credit to Harry.

Having introduced the reader to one or two of my mates, let me tell him more about them, commencing with Bill. He must be first because after all he was the foreman. He used to "rib" me because, as he said, I was "in" with the churchy people. He was of that old school of craftsman that insisted on a good job. If it was not right, then you were told in no uncertain terms and in

15

unprintable language that if you expected to get 2d an hour then you had to earn it. His well-chewed tobacco (Hearts of Oak) was deposited on the floor just under his bench vice. It formed over the years a thick wad of hard cake, brown in colour and similar to those "cakes" which can be seen in a field where cows have grazed. He didn't like it one bit when I told him this. I was sent out of the workshop for a few weeks until I had learnt some manners. When I returned one of my first tasks was to thoroughly sweep and clean up the shop whilst he went out. I really did clean up the shop, including his sacred wad. What he said on his return will never be printed by a publisher of religious books, and his description of me left doubts as to my legitimacy. Poor old Bill, in spite of all his strange ways, had many virtues. His loyalty to the firm, his accuracy, his care for his family, and the encouragement he gave to his daughter were among them. His daughter became a very successful art teacher at the art school where I qualified in teaching art subjects later on. Image my surprise when one evening Miss Wood, while helping me with monotone colour work, said "You really must think before you clean up the floor around the foreman's bench."

In 1934 when Bill was over sixty five and Jesse was failing in health, Bill taught himself contract procedure, estimating, accounting and all the administration up to final accounts. Right up to the day when he himself retired he wore his black six-panelled buttoned top hat that showed the grease of over fifty years in the trade. He was a very hard taskmaster, and I remember visiting him when he was ill. It was then that the real Bill shone through "Thanks for coming over to see me" he said, "Keep at it — you'll get there in the end." When I went to Buckingham Palace on 24 February 1981 I thought of Bill. He has, in my opinion, a share of the medal which I received from Her Majesty the Queen.

Small firms in the building industry formed the

background of development in post-war years and ours was no exception. The old tradition of senior apprentices having their share in the training of the juniors carried on. In our shop at a very early age I met Jack Bulman who was an enthusiastic Scouter at the Methodist Church I had joined. Every Sunday at Wesley the scouts occupied one pew across the centre of the church. Needless to say, the older girl guides were not far away, and after the service we would all make our way to the sea front, where the lads admired not only the white cliffs of Dover, but — I'll leave the rest to you the reader. I was searching for something — a sort of quest which goes on in the mind of most youngsters.

Jack organised us into a football team known as the 7th Dover Rovers. During the week there was a youth club and we Rovers took our turn in providing an evening for the boys who were about twelve years of age. As the years went by they joined the Rovers themselves, and so the whole sequence started again. Jack was one of those young men around whom all things turned. The church sale of work found him busy — and us — fixing up the tables and getting the event into shape. We were all there on the day, including the guides who did the selling. I recall at the time there was one, Edith Worsefold, who was Jack's opposite number with the girls. I wonder where she is now? I haven't heard of her for years. The life, then, for us teenagers was most pleasant, until one day something happened. Jack, our king-pin, became a victim of that dreaded disease, TB. For him it was terminal. We visited him regularly at his home, and almost to the end of his life he continued to organise us, and through courage maintained our group. A few days before his death he told us to keep the group going, and that when we played the coming Saturday's football match we were to go out and win. We did, but Jack was not with us. He died on the Friday. I helped to make his coffin, put him in it, and was a bearer at the funeral. The young apprentice became a senior and began to put all the chips together. We all have a task in God's world, a race to run; and when it's finished He will say "Well done." Many of us from those days still remember Jack and the example he set, and it may be that part of his task in life was to set the standard for those who remained.

Rod Foster, our Padre

Rod was our minister at Wesley Hall for most of the time when I was an apprentice at Jesse Morgan's. He came to our camps and jamborees. He trained us and pointed the way to a life which one has never regretted. I believe that he was of the family which founded the gentlemen's clothing firm. Anyway, he always looked smart to me, especially when he came to the camps in very shiny shirts and wore "snazzy" ties. It was Rod who launched the writer into lay preaching. He asked for volunteers to share one evening service and stand in the pulpit to say just what Christ meant to us. To me this indicated that I should sit down and prepare my "mini-sermon." It amounted to about two pages of what I thought I should say to please all the folk who were bound to be there. Just before we entered the church on our special evening, Rod said to us "I don't want any of you to say anything that you don't mean or truly feel." That was it! I screwed up my notes and had to think quickly. My sermon was brief. In fact, I can remember it now. "Christ means more than He did yesterday and I have no doubt that He will mean more tomorrow than He does today." It was hardly a Billy Graham conversion but the end product was my ordination in 1980 as a result of the hard work put in by folk like Rod, Jack, Captain Stevens, the Vicar, my mother, father and, in an interesting way, Bill Wood. God uses many people as His instruments — people of His choice and often not ours. It was during the years 1931 to 1934 that I was able to serve the Methodists at Snargate Street, Lydden and West Hougham.

The pulpit at Snargate Street was one used by John Wesley, so when I preached there I took special care to say only those things that came from the spirit. Should the reader not know what this means, don't worry — you will when it happens to you. I once discussed the question of sermon preparation with a senior Methodist minister — I hasten to add that it was not Rod. I was finding it very time consuming when at the same time I had my studies at the technical school to pursue. A fresh sermon nearly every week took my preparation often far into the night. "Don't worry" he said, "use the same sermon several times and simply change the text". Need I say that this was not the way that Rod taught? So I took little notice.

As a preacher "on trial" I found my richest blessing at the little church known as West Hougham Methodist. This chapel seemed to revolve around the Tanton family, and their devotion to the work was a great inspiration to any young man. The Sunday School in this very small village numbered thirty children, and their results in the Sunday School Union annual examinations were a great credit to all who laboured there. One year I took their Anniversary service and invited the children to bring along a piece of string three feet long. They did, and I then asked them to tie each piece together to form a long cord, which we found did not quite reach right round the chapel. I challenged them to find new children for their school, and at the next visit I made (that was, if they invited me), we would see just how far it might go. I was back there at the invitation of Mrs Tanton some months later. She said that the children had a surprise for me. Well, dear reader, you have guessed correctly. The string was now long enough to go right round the chapel. It was once said that a cup of tea in a Methodist church is the best, and how right they were at West Hougham.

Lydden Methodist Chapel was another little church proud of its Free Church tradition. I remember with what pride they showed me the nail holes, which, they claimed, were made by the Anglicans many years before when they nailed up the chapel door so that the congregation couldn't get in one Sunday way back in the 19th Century. It's not like that any more as the different traditions have grown closer together.

In those days when doors were nailed up what a pity they didn't think about the nails which were used to fasten a man to a cross. He wanted His people to be one. In my little church at Much Hadham in Hertfordshire we are one, regardless of the particular tradition. Unity we have, Uniformity neither of us want. After all, when you consider it, the Apostles were hardly uniform, but they were most certainly united. The day is long overdue when Christians look beyond the "ists" and "isms" and see only the Carpenter of Nazareth. This work which I call "Chips on the Floor" is not intended to be too much of a sermon but if you, the reader, are an ordinary sort of person (and you must be if you've read this far) you will know what I mean.

I have written a fair amount about folk of the highly respected variety, so now I want to tell you about one who was the living example of the Samaritan. Many folk did not like the way Chris drank to excess especially on Friday, our payday. He was hard-swearing, very coarse in speech, and didn't seem to wash very often. More often than not, in his pocket was a bottle of his favourite brew. His scrammy (food at work) was an enormous slice of bread and the biggest hunk of cheese that you ever saw. "Respectable" folk would avoid him at all costs. A labourer's pay was very small in those days, so poor old Chris wore his working jacket and trousers which were tied up with string just below the knees, until they practically dropped off. My mother once tied up a parcel of old jackets and told me to give them to Chris, and she said to me, "You know, there's something good about Chris." I couldn't then understand what she meant, but I was to discover that for myself shortly afterwards. With the parcel I went round to the public house where I was sure he would be.

"Has Chris been in yet", I asked, popping my head round the corner. "Not yet, he's up the garden digging." True, he was — an old lady's garden. My mother was right. On another occasion I had cause to learn something about him which revealed his true nature. One of the apprentices jobs was to take a handcart down to the timber yard and push a heavy load of timber one and a half miles back to the workshop — uphill all the way. It was very hard work indeed, and by the end of the day one was worn out. On the day I recall, the load I had was so big that as the men at the yard let go of the end I was lifted up off the ground. The cart was rebalanced by the yardman and I made my way through the town uphill back to our Elms Vale workshop. On these timber fetching days it was the nearest I ever came to being a two-legged horse. The halfway rest was near a corner, the equivalent of a lay-by. Coming towards me, walking to the town, was a member of my old church who for some reason looked the other way. I began to think of the Good Samaritan, and wished that one might appear. Even going in the same direction some folk that I knew either slowed up or walked faster when they saw me struggling with the load. After five minutes rest I re-organised the load and started pushing once again. On the other side of the road, walking towards the town, I saw Chris who was on his way to the doctors. Seeing my struggle he came over and the conversation went something like this: "Wo'cher lad, 'aving a bit of a rough ride with that ..... great load? Move over, I'll give you a push back to the ..... yard." In many ways Chris was a Good Samaritan. There are so many like him about, and without them the world would be a poorer place. Chris died a few years ago and there are a lot of ordinary folk who remember him for his qualities, and choose not to recall his weaknesses.

21

Chapter 3

There were many very amusing happenings during an apprenticeship. Some are still clearly in my mind as if it was only yesterday and not forty-eight years ago. Let me tell you about one or two. Jesse Morgan was very strict on the keeping of timesheets by all his employees. We had to write down the job number or name of the client, the number of hours we were engaged on the work, a description of what work we did and the materials that were used. A summary of this eventually appeared on the client's account, and from the information on the timesheets Jesse was able to give estimates for other work as it came along. In a way, you might think of it as a sort of time and motion study, or the beginnings of a "critical path-planning system." There are many fancy names now for what in our day we often called — "'ow long it took, what we done, and what we're gonna do tomorrer." Terrible English but that is the way it was described.

Jesse one morning told me to take a small plane along to Mrs Overy, who was a very special client. She always had a least two rooms papered every winter, and was a good payer. "She's got a large oak chest of drawers," said Jesse, "and dampness has made them bind a bit. Do what you can to keep her happy." I was back in the workshop in an hour, and that included a cup of coffee and a bun. It was at the end of the week that Jesse, looking very serious, came up to me at my bench and said, "Now, young Joe, I want to know that it is you have been up to, if I've read your timesheet correctly". I had written "Monday — two hours taking a little bit off Mrs Overy's drawers." I leave the reader to imagine how long it took to live that down.

In those craftsmanship days, long before plastic came on the scene, we used to make toilet seats from short ends of elm left over from the "box making". Bill had his special pattern to which we had to shape the seat. There were to be no knots or rough bits on the critical part of the seat; it was to be glasspapered smooth, and any sharp corners removed. I thought that Bill's orders for a Loo seat were precise but, as he pointed out, the firm did not want to be sued for damages on account of blisters or boils caused through rough work. This advanced technology of 1934 did amuse me, and again the reaction of Jesse to my timesheet was to be remembered as he read it over to me on payday. I had written "Making stock seats for the lav and testing same." Jesse said in that dry tone of his, "How long did you sit on them Joe? — cause you don't get paid for sitting down."

To mention one more amusing incident. Jack Hogg was the general foreman (he wore a bowler hat) and by trade a bricklayer. He always seemed to "have it in" for the carpenters. Strange, but we could never find him for 11.00 a.m. to 12.30. He would tell us that he had some measuring to do. He did — but it was in pints and certainly not in feet and inches. By 12.45 he would return looking a bit confused and "sunburnt" — in the middle of winter! To show the lads how friendly he wanted to be he would help himself to our chocolate and tell us how good it was to share things with others. (We thought; so long as it's not his things that are shared). For a laugh one day we put some Ex-Lax in a Cadbury's wrapper and laid it where he could see it and, we hoped, succumb to temptation. As well, we nailed up the door of the toilet and put glue on the seat for good measure. Never did we see such a frantic foreman going mad as he wrestled with the door and later emerge. I'll leave the rest to your imagination. He never found out who the culprits were and, alas, poor old Jack never will. He died many years ago. During my first spell on the building site he once sent me off with a large bucket to bring him two gallons of "air space" for a cavity wall. He said it was quite near the air bricks in the store. I never did find it! That's how one learns in the trade.

Perhaps the reader will think that I have treated the trade too lightly. So on the more serious side remember this: the trade in those days was made up of men who were proud of the work they did. They were not cowboys here today and gone tomorrow; they were men of character, and many of those now occupy positions in the ivory towers of the large corporations which have SW1 as the centre of their profession. Many of them must occasionally think back to the days of the handcart, the hand mortice machine and that stinking glue pot as it burnt on the gas ring in the corner. For me they were happy days, and I remember them often when in my pulpit. By the way, I must take some glasspaper with me next Sunday — there's a rough spot on the edge of the lectern!

I have deliberately not written much so far about my technical college training because this in itself forms a period worth separate record. Few of my early associates had much time for what they called "all this ..... theory stuff." I remember how Mr C Weeds at St Martin's School used to tell us that it was important to study the theory of one's trade as well as the practice. In 1929 I enrolled as an evening student at the Dover Technical Institute to study carpentry and joinery, with art as a second string. Mr H H Jacques was the Principal, a Yorkshireman so typical of that tough clan, and in the first interview, although he did not intend it, he terrified me almost as much as Bill on the first day I joined the firm of Jesse Morgan. It later proved that he was one of the best friends I ever had. His presence, commanded respect and the groundwork he put into the Institute became the foundation of the South East Kent College of Technology.

At the interview he asked me what my ambition was in the building industry. I told him that I wanted to be a teacher of carpentry and joinery. There was quite a long pause, as if he was sizing me up (as indeed he was), and he replied, "I will do what I can, but by gum you'll have to work lad." I signed up for five evenings a week to study, much to my dismay, geometrical drawing, mathematics, art, science, English and just one hour of woodwork. My mother and father bought me a bureau, which I still have, father provided an attache case — and behold, I was a student — for five evenings a week. Many of my other evening interests just had to stand aside unless I could find time for them either before the class or afterwards. What was to follow was a period of work hard, play hard and study hard. In order to qualify as a woodwork teacher one had first to gain a high standard of general education in related technology; and above all to be able to speak and write well was essential. It look me a long time to appreciate this, and it was the painstaking labours of Miss Elsie Hughes that helped to achieve this standard. She taught a class of fifteen, mainly boys, who all thought that to read poetry in front of the class was a waste of good woodworking time. She insisted that when she had made what she called her academic "break through" all else would fall into place quite naturally. It was over a year before that break through came. I was reading Walter de la Mare's "When Music Plays." I was spellbound as the poem expressed all that I felt, and I was truly "gone from this world." By now she must be elderly, but if she does ever read this tribute to her teaching skills she will understand when she learns that the writer now writes his own hymn if the one in the book does not match the need. Few good teachers see the real harvest of the seeds they sow in the classroom. If they do, they are richly rewarded.

Mathematics was never my best subject at school, although I did like having "a go." One teacher, Mr Darby, who during the day was a teacher at the Dover

Grammar School for Boys, I especially remember. We boys thought he was a genius because in the prospectus it had after his name the letters BSc (inter). His genius was in qualities rather than mathematics. In wading through the book which dealt with clocks, I came across a problem. It was this: at what time do the hands of the clock lie exactly over each other between the hours of three and four? (Try it, reader — but there now, you are probably good at maths). Mr Darby sat himself down beside me and said, "Let us ask ourselves what it is we know about the background to the problem and then work from there." (If the reader can solve this, OK. If not, drop me a line via the publisher of this book and I'll send the solution to you. SAE please; unless the postage goes down to a twopenny stamp). The patience of Mr Darby knew no end, and to him must go the credit for my success after two attempts in the City and Guilds Handicraft Examination. Throughout my teaching career I always had a class of mathematics. Now I knew their problems, and my opening words were always "Let us ask ourselves what it is..." Shades of Mr Darby! I think it was in 1946 that Edith and I visited a garden party at the Methodist Church at River, near Dover. Browsing over a bookstall I saw an elderly gentlemen who I thought was Mr Darby. Through my mind went the thought "No, it can't be, it was ages ago that I knew him". I walked over to him. "Excuse me Sir, are you Mr Darby?" He adjusted his glasses, looked at me and said, "That's right. You are Smith with a maths problem." He told me that whenever we asked him to help with a problem it was for him just as much a problem at the time, and that maths was never his best subject! And we all thought him a genius. He was a wonderful teacher.

The one evening at the Art School provided release from the brain searching of mathematics and technology (by the way, reader, they called it technology rather than theory to jazz it up a bit. It sounds better and pays more!).

At home in Dover 1928 — outside 11 Lascalles Road

I always liked painting, sketching and enjoying myself in art work, but did not realise that Mr Jacques and Miss Wood were preparing me for the Art Teacher's Certificate Examination, which it was thought might be a good second subject to woodwork. Money was in short supply, especially to an apprentice. The fee for the examination was £1, and too proud to ask my father and mother, I withdrew my name from the list of candidates. Mr Jacques sent for me (it was like a command from the Palace) so I went along to his office. I knocked at the door and a voice boomed out, "Come in, Smith, and sit down. I have a few words to say to you." In no uncertain words he tore a strip off me. "If, one day, you are coming on to my staff, then this stupid sort of pride will have to go. When you have any problems, no matter what they are, you come and see me. You are broke, are you? Well, I too have been hard up. Now go back to your class and take the exam. And by the way, pass it 'cause the fee has been paid and here is the receipt." I did later on join his staff, and there will be more about that later on in this work.

Chapter 4

Thanks to the work of the staff I did pass the art exam, the handicraft exam and the City and Guilds exam in carpentry and joinery. I also passed the Carpenters Institute exam, and as all this brought my apprenticeship years to an end the time was right to search for fresh fields. Where to? Why, London of course, or near to it — but how did one make contacts for such an adventure in those days? London seemed so very far away from Dover, so I asked Mr Jacques. This pleased him, and he advised me to just go there, find a job and digs, and if I was near Watford he would arrange for me to serve as a supernumerary teacher at the Queens Road Technical Institute. Lucky for me, I had friends in Watford and the contacts which were to reshape my life. Loaded with tools and all my gear, I set off for the big new world north of the Thames. Mr Arthur Creed, secretary to ASW in Watford, suggested that the firm, Allensor Ltd, might to able to fit in one more joiner in their large Watford shop. So, with digs organised, and a job, I was away.

The journey to London was uneventful, although as the train moved away from the sea there was a peculiar lump in my throat. It must have been the apple which my mother gave me just before I left. On arrival at Charing Cross, the problems began. How did one get across London with the mountain of luggage that I had brought? The taxi which I thought might take me to the nearest station on the Bakerloo Line was driven by one who said he thought I had ..... cheek to think that his taxi was a lorry. Anyway, by leaving some cases in the left luggage department and taking enough to get by for a day or two, I had my first real experience of a moving staircase, with three bags making life difficult. I stayed for some time with Mrs Kendall, of Eastcourt Road, Watford and felt quite important — truly paddling my own canoe. I collected the rest of my luggage in two or three stages and learned moving the hard way.

Mr Arthur Creed arranged for me to be interviewed at Allensors Ltd, of Kings George's Avenue, and I was taken on as an Improver. There were over thirty joiners in the shop and all around me there seemed to be mountains of wood in all shapes and sizes. Joiners were not expected to leave their bench to sort out material; this was all done by men from another area. My first job was to assemble sashes for a job known as Rod No. 108. There was really not much to do except to glue the joints, put the sash into a multiple cramp, and Bingo! it was done. All my efforts then went to the sandpaper machine for finishing off. On this mass production job each of us did one small part of the work. I did not like this because you took over from one man and never had the pleasure of seeing a task through from start to finish.

It did not take Mr Jeffs long to arrange for me to move position near to Arthur Cox, a very clever craftsman, who specialised in staircases. Arthur was indeed a perfectionist — he still is. From him I was shown the art of preparing wood for the french polisher and making those beautiful staircases which are to be seen in banks and public buildings. You know, the sort of expensive things which somebody else pays for. Allensors produced work of the highest standard, and to be able to say that you had been on the bench there, was as good as a qualification. Something like a lad who can boast that he had been trained at Kew. I found this out later when I applied for a job elsewhere. Mention Allensors and you were in. Firms didn't even want to see certificates; for them it was what can you do — not what do you know. I recall the wonderful craftsmen I met and who helped me at

Allensors. Let me name them, because in my book they rate high: Billy Crew, Jack Dorer, Ted Hanchet, Tommy Trinder (not the one from Fulham), Tom Chase, Bert Blundell, Cox senior, who was Arthur's father and the firm's measurer (they would call him a quantity surveyor today). As I became more "dug in" and accustomed to this new world of woodworking, which was far removed from Jesse Morgan's shop, I knew that advice given to me by Mr Jacques was sound. It was soon discovered that I attended the little mission hall in Meeting Alley, Watford, and occasionally there was the gentle leg-pull. In conversation I must have revealed my early lay-preaching days at Dover. When it was known that another improver was to join the staff, one David Mockford who was the son of a Baptist Minister, I was asked if we could share the same bench.

On the notice board one morning there appeared where I couldn't miss seeing it a large poster on which was written:

TODAY!! SPECIAL AT LUNCHTIME
BROTHER SMITH WILL "SPOUT"
AT OUR FIRST BIBLE CLASS
BROTHER MOCKFORD WILL
READ TO US

It was intended as a first-class laugh. I moved over to my bench and David, who was by nature of a nervous disposition, said "Oh dear, what are we going to do?" "Exactly what is on the notice." The "legpullers" had found a New Testament in the yard and had placed it on my bench. We selected for the reading the Sermon of the Mount. Use the words of Christ and you cannot go wrong. It's when sectarians pick out bits to suit themselves that things go wrong. (One member of parliament might take a note of this comment). At lunchtime, having eaten our sandwiches in between glue sessions earlier in the morning, we moved in ready for the fray. I opened the meeting with a prayer in which God was thanked for making the meeting possible through those who had made the poster. There was hush. They were told that whether they liked it or not they were daily occupied in a trade which was chosen by God. They accepted the trade as theirs, so why not go further? David read to the men and here was perhaps the beginning of Works Fellowship — not anything official or smiled upon by the Rural Dean. It just happened, and with what results! Just before the buzzer was due to go, signifying the return to work, at least five of the joiners came up to say, as if they were a bit ashamed of it, that they were regular members of local churches or chapels (take your pick, 'cause church or chapel, they are both the same to me). To the reader I say, reverently, "For Christ's sake, don't be ashamed of your belief." You need not bulldoze folk into your way but share His way.

Not long after service I found myself made the sick visitor for the ASW branch. For this struggling Christian, life was becoming interesting, to say the least. It turned out that it was someone who professed to be an agnostic who made out the poster. Isn't it amazing whom God uses! A long time ago it was some fishermen, and only a few centuries ago it was the captain of a slave-trading ship. Perhaps you, the reader, knows all the answers. I don't!

With my job sorted out and good digs, I looked for a church into which I could put some effort. There was not much money left after paying for my keep, and I had to save enough to pay for my visit home to mother and father, and to see old friends. I walked on the Sunday to Queens Road, Watford, intending to go to the Methodist Church, but to my dismay I found outside the church a huge notice saying "SILVER COLLECTION, Sunday, 6.30 p.m." I had read somewhere about a "mite." I couldn't figure it out, so I continued towards Beeching Grove and Meeting Alley. It was about 6.25, as I was passing the car park, that I saw a grand old gentlemen standing outside the Watford Gospel Mission. Seeing me, he said, "You're just in time, do come in." He was Mr Brice. He had a marvellous white beard and — well, who could refuse him? The leader of this little mission was Mr L C Johnson, and in the notices for the day he said that they needed a leader for the youth work, preferably a man who had experience in woodwork. This was it! A direct challenge, and who could refuse? The following Monday found me meeting the lads who lived near Meeting Alley, to start their club off. Boxing was the sport which appealed to these tough little lads, so, linking up with one Hughie Rowlinson, a little stocky Welshman who was quite a boxer, I and Hughie showed the boys how to spar and parry. This was fun for weeks, until I swung him a sly one — he responded suitably — and from then my pugilistic career came to an excruciating end — .....

One lad, Leslie Grubb, who was affectionately known as "Fatty" (he was!), also came to the Mission on Sundays. I asked my group to write out a composition entitled, "Things I enjoy doing." Fatty, whose plump little hands could hardly hold a pencil, produced a most beautiful script in a copperplate style. "Did you do this?" "Yes sir, all by myself." "Honestly?" "Well, he used my pencil." I am told that Fatty died during the war.

It was at the Mission, when the choir, under Mr Emerton, were giving us some special rendering, that the choir filed into their seats and I looked at the "prospects." In case you do not understand the word, in this situation it means young ladies. One in particular struck me as the answer to a young man's wildest dreams. My thoughts were: "I am going to marry that one." We did marry three years later in the same mission hall. During the three years at the mission I was able to serve on the committee and did a short spell as the secretary. It provided a training ground for more pulpit service and the realisation that the ministry is not the preserve only of those who wear the cloth. In certain areas this mission hall may have been regarded as the church of the lesser fry — not quite in the record of establishment — of these little places, and there are still plenty of them about, I am glad to say. I think they are the backbone of the church and the right spiritual home for many very ordinary folk, of which I am proud to be one.

There came a time when Allensors had little work, and it looked as if there would have to be a lay-off for many of the men. Those of us who were unmarried decided to try London and broaden our experience in the trade. There was good money to be earned there; so off we went to start again. I found a job with Harry Neal Ltd of Northwood Hills, at Forsett Court in the Edgware Road. It was a huge block of flats and gave me a whole new range of experience in the trade, and, incidentally, in sociology. I say sociology because education receives its hall mark only in the big cities. It is there you rise or fall, and believe me a large city can be ruthless. I'll tell you a little about it.

I teamed with Harry Hughes who also originated from Dover. We were taken on at the Edgware Road job on what is termed second fixing and finishing. We knew that the job was likely to last only a few weeks and expected to "get the bullet" after we had completed it. It was the accepted practice to slow up a bit near the end of the job unless you found something in the meantime. However, we kept going — after all, a fair day's work for a fair day's pay was the way we had both been trained. The site "king" realised that he had two good types and put us both over to Haymarket on the Steam Sentinel Waggon new office site next to the Haymarket Theatre. There was a huge penalty clause in the contract for failure to complete on time, and we were told that if we wanted to earn big money it was there for the taking; if we wished we could work round the clock and snatch a few winks — so long as the job came out to time; that was all that mattered. We took this up and at midnight on the first day we decided to find an eating place, even though it was in the middle of the night. We were told that just off Haymarket there was a night cafe. We tracked it down and looked around for the waiter — they were around in those days to serve you. An oily looking character came over to us and asked if we wanted the meal first or after. This was a bit puzzling, so we asked him "after what?" With a roar of coarse laughter he pointed to the table in the corner where sat females whose purpose was quite clear. Eventually we did find a good place under the arches near Charing Cross. In the first place of doubtful reputation it was taken for granted that eating was purely for energy building but not for working on the site. There they gambled for women and boys; but believe this, in the day time a complete change of staff made the place into a perfectly respectable eating house. We never returned to that area because if it was thought that we were "narks" there was every chance of being "looked over" or "roughed up". Working next to us were wife swappers who quite openly arranged their weekends (we were even offered a share) and they just could not understand us when we expressed our views on their activity. It was often best, if you wanted to keep you nose in one piece, to keep it clean. The grape-vine used to tell us about jobs where there had been very nasty accidents, and rapid promotions to other jobs for those who didn't see a thing. There was the plasterer who suffered a burn caused by an electrical fault on temporary wiring. We heard that he did recover quite quickly, and of all things, was made an area manager. It was so easy to accept bribes and "work the dead man" swindle. In spite of all this, when it was made clear where you stood in relation to this life you were respected and not pressed. One man near to us in the site always "hocked" his best suit on Monday morning and redeemed it on payday. One character told us that the best plugs to use for fixing after you made the hole with a rawplug was a bit of well-chewed tobacco! Harry and I worked four days and nights (just the odd rest), and picked up at the end of the week the equivalent to five weeks' wages.

For two evenings a week during most of my stay in Watford I attended the evening institute to study physics, and on one of the evenings helped Mr H Mellon, the woodwork teacher, as a supernumerary. With a busy life in the daytime, my church on Sunday, the studies to continue, and a girl friend to keep happy, my life was full to capacity. It became necessary for me to gain some experience in another field, if eventually I was to enter a full-time teaching job. I chose to apply for a post at Cox and Company off the Watford Bypass. After a test I was appointed as their first template and pattern maker. As a member of the staff and not "that rough old lot on the factory floor," I was allowed to have my meals in the staff restaurant, not in the canteen. Oh, by the way, the managerial staff had their food behind a screen and had table cloths. In case you don't know, the latter are now the special preserve of Clive Jenkins. In this wonderful age of greater equality, I hope he campaigns for table cloths on the canteen tables 'cause I believe that very few workmen these days eat off the pages of "The Sun" — or do they?

Quite unexpectedly illness struck me — serious illness — I found myself going home to Dover, where the quieter scene of the home town was to have its recuperative effect, together with that care that only mothers can give. Good care, the fresh air of Dover, and some fishing off the pier, soon resulted in recovery and fitness for work. Quite near to my home was a builder, who in many ways reminded me of my early days at Jesse Morgan's workshop, and he wanted a foreman carpenter. By trade Mr Dolbear was a bricklayer, and on the Maxton Estate he was developing an estate of some two hundred houses. To test me out he asked me to set out the land for a pair of semi-detached houses. He must have been satisfied because I was offered the job. He was a very firm but fair employer and helped

36

me tremendously to develop those skills which made for leadership in the industry. He often asked me to take home plans from which the quantities were extracted, or he would take a chance in letting me make an estimate for a small contract. I felt something like a technical Bill Wood, although I can assure you that at the end of the bench walk there was no "baccer wad", and it was my apprentice who swept up the chips on the floor.

Edith came down from Watford to stay with us and on our visits to the town we were able to work out our future and name the day. We chose June 7th 1939, and to start off properly we settled for the purchase of one of the houses on the estate. I believe it was at a price difficult to believe in these days of 1981 — wait for it — £550. We were married at the Mission and the reception was in Queens Road at Pearces. What a day it was! Blazing hot and sunny. We set off in the evening for the return to Dover and our own home in Farthinglow Road. A good name, Farthinglow, because everything paid for, a honeymoon was out of the question. It was about eleven at night when the taxi dropped us outside the house, and true to tradition, I lifted my bride to carry her over the threshold, believing that we had this all to ourselves — but wait a moment — the neighbours were all ready. Windows came open and cheers were heard along the road. Back to work on Monday and Edith commenced her homekeeping, working out to a fine art how to budget on £3/10/0d a week. If you are only metric-minded that is about £3.50p. At the end of the day, what with mortgage, rates and food, there was only 2/6d (12½p) for pocket money.

Out of the blue one day arrived a letter from Mr Jacques in which he said that he had monitored my adventures in London and Watford, and my return to Dover, and he also mentioned the fact that now I was married I might like to visit him and have a chat about the future.

It was about the same time that a man in Germany had

designs about his future. Thundering nerve he had! He was a house painter in Berlin. In the town, house sales were slow and the Government of the day became worried. We found ourselves building air-raid shelters and making extra strong doors for the caves at the foot of the white cliffs. People were joining the ARP and learning about first aid. Edith and I were anxious as the dark clouds appeared on the horizon. That September we were building warden's posts at key places in the town, and instructions were given to those of us in the ARP about what to do in the event of the worst happening. It did — on September 3rd when we heard the news that was to turn the world upside down.

As a struggling Christian many great decisions had to be made. Edith and I talked about them and prayed about them. It's not very easy to say a prayer when you cannot be sure that you will be able to finish it. The threat of air-raids or shells is a bit disturbing to young newly-weds. Just imagine going to bed with your wellies at the bedside and your gas mask on the dressing table!

Whilst working in Snargate Street one Sunday morning I stood on a wall which was part of the warden's post and noticed a ship pulling in to the quay-side. Nothing unusual about that — ships did every day. But this ship had on board wounded and tired soldiers. Dunkirk! They were the advance party of the army of thousands which fought its way back to England, and all this was the devilish work of that ..... painter from Berlin. Why didn't he keep to stopping up, priming, undercoating and finishing a good gloss paint? If he had he wouldn't have ended up in a German bunker, guilty of the deaths of millions who would have been quite content to be just ordinary folk.

I volunteered to join up and sort this man out. At Canterbury a Major gave me a shilling (that was handy) and I was a sapper awaiting orders. It puzzled me why they didn't send for me straight away — when one is young patience is not often a virtue. However, when I was convinced that they did not really want me the orders came, together with a railway warrant for Chester. Edith was wonderful about all this upset. To keep our home we put all the furniture into one room and let our house to a young couple. Edith went to her home in Watford, and I made tracks for the training area at Hough Green, Chester. In reflection it was as if our world had been split in two and all our plans were changed. It is a good thing that we do not always know what tomorrow will bring. "Take no thought for the morrow — what it will bring." It is not our will that will be done, and after all it's better that way.

There was one problem, however. After all my expenses had been paid I found that I had just sixpence (or 2½p) left! In survival we do not count the cost. At the end of the war we would (DV) start all over again and put the pieces together again, but how much was to happen in the meantime! In the next chapter I will write about the adventures of 1885714 Sapper J J Smith, who believed that evil must be destroyed and the *weak* defended. If you wish, substitute the word "disadvantaged" for "weak" and you have what the same sapper believes today. There will be many "philosophers" who will tear my thesis to pieces. They may do this if they wish, but watch out if they do it and hurt someone in so doing.

Chapter 5

The wonderful folk of Chester did far more than was expected of them in accepting lads from all over England. I was first billeted on Mrs Lynch in Saltney — a lady just like my mother in the way that she cared. Then I was moved to the home of Mr and Mrs Massey of 21, Victoria Road, Saltney. "Mass" treated me as one of her family, and forty one years later we still write and keep in touch. Thank God some people were made like her. I'll tell you more about them, as I am sure she will not mind, nor will those good folk who ran a coffee evening for the troops at the Methodist Church — we called it Smokey Joes.

One of the most important NCOs in a training battalion is the Lance Corporal. He takes a civilian raw recruit, and with a system of cutting down to size, withdrawing all identity, barking, pushing, shoving, and superb example, produces a soldier. At first our reaction was one of "Oh Hell — let Jerry come — it cannot be worse than this." But just when all are in a state of surrender to anything the Corporal says, a word of praise from him restores morale, and off you go to learn that even if you wanted to you cannot beat the man in front, wearing — just one stripe. Our Lance Corporal Bulmer was a first-class soldier and in three weeks changed our motley company into Sappers who found themselves proud of the corps. We did not see quite so much of the Sergeant, but he was there somewhere, keeping his beady eye on us. One Saturday we were formed up by the Corporal, who said that the Sergeant was coming to speak to us.

"COMPANY-Y-Y-Y-Y, atten-SHUN!!!" We were frozen solid. He looked at us and gave the command,

40

"Stand at ease." We thawed out a little.

"Tomorrow, in case you don't know, is Sunday; and as you lot are just about smart enough to go to the house of the Almighty you will form up outside of Hough Green Methodist Church — that is, unless you are detailed for the C. of E. If any of you are agnostic then you will report to the cookhouse for a whole day of spud bashing." There was not a lot of choice really, when you had helped in the morning to unload six hundredweight of potatoes. Church parade was to be at 10.30 outside the church. I had already for weeks attended the church and had on one occasion taken their service as their own laymen were in the services elsewhere in the country; so my first service as part of an army unit was to be an unusual experience. Before we were dismissed the Sergeant said, "There's one thing more for you sappers. Whoever it is that stands in the pulpit represents the Almighty 'imself and whatever 'e says goes; and I don't want to 'ear about any buttons being found in the plate when I go to the prayer meeting to sort you lot out! PARADE, dismiss!!" The orders were quite clear and on the Sunday morning we were ready for the entry into the church. Frankly, as I looked round I did think that our turnout was good — it had to be! We filed into the church and sat down — after the NCOs had seated themselves where there were cushions and behind the lads so that they could keep an eye on them. I found a place at the end of the a pew and we all waited for the minister to take his place in the pulpit. By 11.05 he had not arrived and I noticed that the steward was looking a little worried. I took a chance and asked him if anything was wrong. At 11.15 he came to me and said that the minister had come off his motor cycle and would not be able to conduct the service — would I do it? Well, I replied, if the Sergeant gives permission, I'll do it.

A most worried Sergeant gave his permission and I found myself in the vestry changing one or two of the hymns so that my mates could have a good sing. I did hope they would not let me down — and they didn't. I could not even hear the parodies that soldiers so often sing to the well-known tunes. The sermon was short and my text for this wonderful opportunity was "Judge not, lest thou be judged." It pleased the boys, but I was not too sure of the Sergeant's reaction. Now here is the punch line of the story. As I stood at the door to shake hands with the congregation I remembered what the Sergeant had said about the person in the pulpit; and then as he came towards me I said, "How nice it was, Sergeant, to see you and your men here this morning. Do come along to our prayer meeting and service next week." I will never forget the look on his face when, after it was all over, I marched over to him and said, "Permission to fall in, Sir." He was well respected by the boys and at the end of training he won our affection. On the last evening in Chester he had organised with "The Last Pub in England" on the English side of the level crossing, to entertain us with sandwiches made and given by the hosts. Tea, beer and even a glass of milk if that was our choice. We all sat down expectantly as the food was brought in. The Sergeant rose to his feet. "All you Sappers, pay attention for a moment. Before we eat and drink this evening I will ask the Bishop to say Grace." We sat there wondering if the Bishop of Chester had been invited. Then he looked in my direction. "Sapper Smith! on your feet and thank the good Lord for all this food and drink." Bless him, he was a great man, our Sergeant; the Corporal too.

Edith joined me in Chester for a short time before I was posted to Chatham. Mr and Mrs Massey made their room available to us. In a way it was like a belated honeymoon — happiness — but we knew that after a little more training we would be parted for a long time. Edith returned to Dover and I moved to the Depot at Chatham. I reached there in the blackout, and in the middle of an air-raid. What a welcome! I was very tired and it was "head down" as soon as I found a place.

What was it that took me to this training depot of great fame? It all began a week before we were passed out in Chester as Sappers. In the last week of our training we were put on to the assault course, which required us to do the most extraordinary things, like climbing a cliff with the instructors throwing things at us, as well as calling us everything under the sun to rattle us; and football matches between "B" and "C" Companies, and on into a final at which the excitement could only be matched at Wembley. In one of the games leading to the semi-final I was not selected to play as I was not good enough, so they let me take along a first-aid kit just in case there was an accident. There was, and what an experience I had, and what an outcome!

At the beginning of the second half we were losing 2 – 0 and tension ran high. I don't know why it should 'cause there was a war on and frankly whoever won we were soon to be all mixed up when we were posted to our next unit. Anderson our left wing "Springbok" ran down the field and a goal looked certain. We were all cheering him on — Pass man!! *Pass*!! Shoot! Then it happened — he slipped, put out his arm as he fell and stayed down — injured. My big chance had arrived. Across the field, down on one knee and a quick look. He had fractured his collar bone. I knew that because of the shortening and his position. The gas mask case provided the fulcrum and a broad bandage maintained bone position as they removed him from the field on a stretcher. I raced across to the MO's room where I knew that an ambulance could be obtained to take the man to the military hospital. I knocked on the door — no reply; knocked again and then ventured to peep in through the small glass panel which was used by the MO to look through when he wanted to see how many were on sick parade. Inside I saw a medical orderly (a lance-jack), feet up on the MO's table, reading "No Orchids for Miss Blandish," and sitting in the MO's chair. That was it! I opened the door, walked in, and what followed was to change my military career.

Lance-jack, rising like a barrage balloon: "Sapper, what the ..... hell do you think you are ..... doing here."

"I want an ambulance for my casualty, Sir."

"You .....!! young ..... Sapper — want an ambulance!"

"And I want it soon, Sir."

"You are on a charge."

"Never mind — make it worthwhile and get up off your backside, put that rubbish away and do your job properly. Show a little more respect for the MO's office."

That was it, this character just about blew up like a charge of dynamite. In fact, there are not enough tabs on my typewriter to do justice to his vituperative after-blast. I picked up the 'phone, called for an ambulance and made a hasty exit in case the Corporal needed transport to the mortuary (for him, of course). As I helped to put Anderson on board the cooled-off Corporal ordered me off the ambulance. He had planned my close arrest. Taking no notice, I went to the hospital and was able to give the MOD an accurate case-history (less my share with the "Blandish fan"). I thought the whole incident had blown over nicely, but the services do not work that way. Next day on the first parade the company officer, Lt. Nobbs said "Fall out the following: Adams, Casbolt (my mate! What's he done?), Dean," and so on through the lot of us in alphabetical order, until — "SMITH!!!" That was it. He dealt with all the others and then told me to report to his office. Once in the office — "Sit down, Smith. I have two reports on you here: one is a charge sheet and the other is a letter from the hospital commending you highly for prompt action at the match on Sunday. What have you to say?" I explained. "Well," he said, "You have put me in a spot — and this is what I want you to do." Thoughts of spud bashing came to my mind, and even worse — floor scrubbing!!! "Apply to me in writing for a course of training as clerk of works. It means that you will be off quickly to Chatham — and good luck. Dismissed, and apologise to the Corporal." Faces were saved all round, and I was off to the SME Chatham. That in itself was like a "gong."

Before being accepted officially for the course at Chatham we had to pass a test of general building knowledge. It was a multiple test-paper on which there were 100 questions — which just about covered the work I had done at Dover several years before under the watchful eye of Mr Jacques. The candidates simply sat down and ploughed their way through the paper until they had exhausted their knowledge. It was a well designed paper and had been prepared by Staff Sergeant Bragg of the SME staff. It seemed that 75% was the required pass mark. Anyway, that was all I could answer and I was accepted for the training course.

Our lectures were constantly interrupted by air-raids, and at one time to cope with the work we had to move frequently from the classroom to the shelter. Drawing in the class and then making haste to the underground shelter, where we carried on with our notes on concrete and road construction, seemed to be quite a routine for us in those perilous days. But without a doubt the course at the SME was good. Throughout the world today you will find engineers working on almost every type of project. Have a few words with them and you will find that they were at one time trained at Chatham. Visit any good technical college and there is an old Sapper lecturing in the field of survey, construction or civil engineering.

My pass mark was 70%. No bad, and as the Staff Sergeant said it could have been better. Promotion to Staff Sergeant followed in a week and we all felt quite pleased wearing our three stripes, crown and a bomb on our sleeves (by the way, not a real bomb, just a fabric one). The regular soldiers did not like us war-time types because their course lasted two years and ours only three months. They did not realise that most of us had been in the trade for years, and in the overall assessment it just about balanced out. All soldiers have something to grouse about, it's a point of principle, most of them don't mean it.

I was depot orderly Sergeant for one week. This was to teach us the ropes of what a senior NCO has to do. It meant that you stayed in, and at 10 p.m. you had to check all personnel in at the gate. There was a long queue drawn up before this time, and every pass had to be carefully checked with the paybook. At 10 p.m. sharp the depot Sergeant Major put down the barrier and told me to put all those on the outside on a "fizzer" — this means a charge if you are a rookie or a civvy. I thought this action was quite unjust as after all they were on time. The depot regular quite adamant. "Book the .....", was his only thought. OK, I mused, I'll check on the depot standing order and see exactly what the score is in these matters, there must be something there to sort him out. There was — it clearly laid down that the Staff Sergeant on duty (that was me) must inspect all rooms and report to the officer for the day any breaches of good discipline, such as untidy room, dust on selves, lights left on, arms left insecurely around, empty cans littering the rooms, etc. etc. — and — this was it — ! — NO PIN UPS OF YOU KNOW WHAT ON THE WALLS. I made my inspection and found in the room of the nasty piece of work who wanted to "peg" everyone that on his walls there was a display that, by today's rating, warranted an X certificate!! I put him on a charge. It worked out all right in the end — nobody was on a "fizzer." In the Sergeants mess there were wry comments made by some of the regulars generally to the effect that "Some of this lot will have to go — and the sooner the better!"

It suited most of us because who wants to hang around the base when there's a war to sort out. Orders came through that all ranks were to be confined to barracks until further orders. I didn't think much about this as I had no intention of absconding, and as I wanted a book from the public library in the town I asked to see Sergeant Major Campion. After all, I was then a Staff Sergeant and surely that was warrant for some privilege. I explained, and he replied, "Fifteen minutes to double there (that means run) and fifteen minutes to double back — ten minutes to select a book. If you are not back here in forty minutes then ..... you're in trouble." I made it but learnt a lesson "Be careful if you want to be smart."

I had one week's embarkation leave with Edith and my parents, and then back to Chatham to wait for a very short time. In the middle of the night, one week later, we were to be off. What an eventful week that was.

Sleeping in the basement of "H" block one night, we heard the drone of an enemy bomber overhead. Not to worry; we were in the basement and thought it to be safe. There was a familiar whining noise, Whee..........ee, then CRASH!! Glass, dust, bits of brick, and shouts of "It's us" filled the room. We were all shaking, and then in the next room we heard the sound of groaning and knew that the bomb had landed right on our mates. In that sort of situation you don't think about any plan of action — you find yourself doing the most unpredictable things.

"Anyone here done first-aid?" — "Yes, mate" — "Get over 'ere quick, we're going in." There was a scramble. "Bring any sheets and blankets — anything that's handy." Six of us went in, and what we saw was little short of bloody hell. A whole building block had collapsed on to our mates; some were already dead and their remains were plastered on the wall, and in some places as we tried to reach those who were groaning, we had to crawl over torn bodies and separate limbs. It was terrifying. I moved towards one bunk and saw, flattened almost to a thickness of three inches, a young Scot whose flesh was pressed into diamond shapes as the wire forming the spring part of the bunk slowly killed him. HE WAS STILL ALIVE! Somehow I managed to get my arm around him and murmur a prayer, "Oh God in Heaven, bring ...." Jock spoke in pain: "Just give me a fag, mate, it's shit or bust for me." I gave him a fag, he took one draw and ..... died in my arms. My watch fell out of my pocket onto his stomach. I didn't know this until the next day when the big sort out came and it was handed back to me. By the way, reader, please excuse the vulgarity in Jock's last words — you have the story exactly as it happened, and the complete language. Now pray that mankind will see the utter senselessness of warfare, and learn that nothing is ever gained by war; and it's mankind that does it. For several days afterwards we slept in the caves until the shock had levelled out. I say, levelled out, but it never really goes. THEY SHALL GROW NOT OLD, AS WE THAT ARE LEFT GROW OLD .... WE SHALL REMEMBER THEM.

Three o'clock in the morning — a hand quietly awakening us and a voice: "Form up outside in twenty minutes, full marching orders — we are moving." So this was it. We boarded the train at Chatham at four in the morning and were soon making up the hours' lost sleep. Some thought it a good opportunity for a hand of cards, but were soon well away. Our troop train never seemed to see the light of day, as so much time was spent in tunnels all the way to Scotland. This was a security measure brought about because someone had known that we were another batch ready for the journey to .... We did not know where we were going to, but we had been issued with tropical clothing.

If you want a good laugh, see me in a large white topee and shorts! In fact, many of us looked like Livingstone himself, except that our knees were still white. We reached Gourack in Scotland in the early hours of the next day — what a journey! On the quayside was a solitary Sally Army girl with a tea and bun waggon. No band, no Major to see us off, and it was even misty as we boarded a tug which took us out to the *SS Leopoldville*, a Belgian ship whose crew had opted to serve the allies in the war effort. Senior NCOs were allocated cabins, and the men were marshalled down below to a system of hammocks, which seemed to me to swing in my direction, showing a pair of feet, every time I passed when doing a spot of duty. There was duty for this and a duty for that; in fact, there was never a dull moment as the days passed.

Making our introductions, the three of us in the cabin decided to plot our course every day, using a small compass and an estimate of the speed the boat was travelling. We had a map of the world in the back of a book which we found in the cabin. Once out of the Clyde we moved north, it seemed for days, and when one morning we found enormous icicles on the ship's rigging we wondered whether the tropical kit was not an error of issue. We plotted west and then south, and were told by the steward that we were only hours from the States. The temperature soon changed from temperate to tropic. The steward then told us that we were now on the equator. Phew! it got hotter and hotter.

One morning there was a great deal of activity on the ship. The swimming pool had been decorated and we were told to be ready to meet Father Neptune in person! We were to be thrown into the pool unless of course we had a certificate from him which would exempt us from the ordeal. Crossing the Line is a tradition that even a "U" boat could not stop. It was good fun, especially when, after fifty of us had been "done", were made into a press gang to seek out those who had tried to dodge the ceremony.

As we made course along the equator in an easterly direction we were able to listen in to the ship's radio. We heard 'Lord Haw Haw' saying, "Where is the *Ark Royal?* Where is the *Ark Royal?*" I will not write what the boys yelled out, but when I say it was less than two miles away from us, you can use your imagination. As we approached Freetown, on the west coast of Africa, the Royal Navy escort pulled away from us and we were on our own as a convoy. We were fairly safe in the South Atlantic and the whole ship took upon itself the tone of a very expensive cruise. One difference — it was even hotter below decks, and at night after an inspection around the hammocks, I then knew why we were told to hang on to our gas mask!

Freetown was one of the most exciting harbours in the world, we thought, and it made a wonderful change from seeing nothing else but sea, flying fish, and an occasional ship, for five weeks. Tropical kit was the order of the day, but it transpired that we had all been issued with the same oversize garments. Talk about the long and the short and the tall! We looked wonderful, and if Hitler's troops had seen us they would have surrendered immediately. Alterations were soon made and we became an orderly-looking army ready for anything. In the harbour the natives paddled out with their "bum boats", loaded with bananas and lush fruit which they sold for a shiny sixpence. One man wrapped up a farthing in silver paper and tried to pass it off as a sixpence in exchange for fruit. The ship's Captain heard about it and the man spent four days in the ship's cooler. He told the native over the tannoy, so that all could hear, that this man was a disgrace to the ship and himself. Justice was done. After Freetown we broke convoy and continued south towards the Cape, on a course just out of sight of land, although any aircraft could have seen us.

One the tenth week of our voyage I got up early one morning to take a walk on deck, opened to the door of the cabin, and — we were at Cape Town!! The table cloth was coming over the plateau and the war seemed a thousand miles away — as it was. Tremendous excitement on board, the officers buzzing about all over the place, and the ship's officers getting ready to see their friends at the port which they must have called at on many occasions before. I wondered what our chances were of getting some shore leave. Over the tannoy came the news: "Any man on board who has relatives or friends in Cape Town can have sleeping-in leave for a week if he applies to the office straightaway." My friends and I had no such luck so we had to do something about finding friends pretty quickly.

Looking longingly out of the porthole of our cabin we could see the quayside, which was alive with officials from the city making all the checks which seemed so necessary every time a liner came to the port. Nearby we spied a staff car and waiting at the wheel was the driver, a lady in uniform who looked to us to be an ATS Sergeant. "Hello there, Sergeant, did you come out from England earlier?" "Oh yes, about twenty years ago!" She looked amused. "Would you befriend three of us, 'cause if you will we can have a week's leave on shore." She looked even more amused and replied "OK, meet me at the dock gates at four when I come off duty." What a stroke of luck for us — we qualified for the special leave concession. Up to the ship's office in double quick time to present our claim. The officer was most interested and asked us if we were hoping to visit relations or friends. When we told him that it was a friend we had, he asked if it was a friend of years' standing, and imagine his look when I said that the friendship was just one hour old. He agreed however, and said something about initiative being the essential of a good soldier. Whatever he said didn't worry us — we had the shore leave promised.

At four o'clock there were three smart Staff Sergeants at the dock gates, who did not have to wait very long. A large staff car pulled up and out jumped our friend. She took us to her home to meet her mother and to tell them what we could of UK news. They proved to be good friends. We were taken to the top of Table Mountain and told about all the things one never did when in the cape. Needless to say, before I had been there very long I broke all the rules in the book. There were several positions where the stamps were sold and we noticed that one of them was apparently ready to serve us as there was no queue. We stood there for a few moments until one of the assistants came along to inform us that we were in the "blacks only" booth. Strange this, because they had exactly the same money as us. After posting our mail we sauntered down

Adelaide Street to find a snack bar where we might buy tea and buns. I stood to one side to let a coloured lady pass with her twin pram. She smiled her thanks and a few yards further on a man tapped me on the shoulder and told me in no uncertain terms that whites never stand to one side for blacks. This puzzled me too, because after all they were there first.

My particular friend was a Maori and we spotted a cafe which looked good. We went in and made our way to the counter. All the other customers then got up and left the cafe. I wondered if we had chosen closing time for our refreshment and apologised to our host. "You needn't apologise," he said, "When you are down here you don't walk into a place like this with a black." Just what sort of society is it that measures people by the colour of their skins? South Africa was supposed to the a Christian country. I wondered whether they knew that Jesus Christ was coloured. This colour prejudice, so I am told, has increased quite a lot in the Cape. If they step out of line now they finish up in prison, and if there are too many of them they "disappear."

It was in Cape Town that my friend and I had our first encounter with violence. One evening whilst sitting on the verandah of a restaurant overlooking the main street we heard a commotion below in the street. There were hundreds of soldiers enjoying the evening air, but in the middle of the crowd two men were fighting. We decided that it was our job to sort them out, especially as one of them, we could see, was from our ship and this could mean that all would lose leave if things got out of hand. Muscling up all the strength that a Sergeant can, we went down to "wade in." Immediately one of the two turned on my friend and the other on me; he was a seaman and produced a knife which to me looked like ending my military career almost before it had started. There was not much option. I gave him the benefit of my size 11 army boot in a place where — use you own imagination. He was still fighting and it remained for me to bring into play all that combat training we had been taught at Chester. It worked, although my wrist came up to an enormous size. The ambulance took the men away to hospital; my friend and I "dissolved" into the crowd, and we made our way back to the ship. Going on board, it meant that we had to pay compliments to the officer for the day, as we reached the top of the gangway. "You have a swollen wrist, Staff — what happened?" "I fell, Sir, as I stepped off the kerb." This I thought would conclude the matter, but, oh no, the next morning the officer on duty passed a comment: "Good job last evening, Staff, you and Kiwi saved the leave."

The week went all too quickly and we were soon back on the ship for the last leg of the voyage — north through the Straits of Madagascar and on to the sight of Zanzibar. Even when two miles from the island you can smell the cloves, which remind one of apple pie. Into the Red Sea and on to Port Toufek. Here we disembarked and after a long drive in the back of a lorry we entered a base camp, tired and ready to sleep. Most of us thought that it was a poor reception party after the long trip we had to play our part in sorting out the enemy — but the enemy had other ideas. A fighter plane came low out of the mist and scorched up the lines of tents, letting fly with all it had. We dived low. No casualties, only one enemy aircraft shot down by the ack-ack.

A couple of days there whilst our future movement was being sorted out found us picking up the first words of Arabic and discovering the delights of "eggs and bread." It's when you feel that you are settling down that the Army moves you, and soon we were off north Alexandria. There I was posted to the CRE office to understudy a Staff Sergeant who was to be posted home. He had been in Alex for several years and had created a little private empire. We heard about the war in the Western Desert and met men who came back with their tales of advance and retreat. Just about a mile from where my office was situated a Royal Navy ship was attacked by Italian frogmen — and by the way they were the very first frogmen in war operations, very brave men indeed. During the evenings I was able to explore Alex and learn the meaning of the expression "Ice-cold in Alex". On days off, to swim and bathe in the Med off Alex was a delight in the extreme — the water was lukewarm. We were enjoying this, and again, as we thought, this is a place for keeps, a posting order came through.

By rail to Sarafand in Palestine where there was an enormous base depot. To me it seemed that the whole of the British Army were there. Shops, cinemas, churches, clubs and scores of military police to keep us all in order. To this camp came thousands of men from Australia, New Zealand, South Africa, Canada; it was like a League of Nations assembly point. Apart from the occasional duty turn there was little to do but wait. It was there that an association and ensuing friendship was made which has lasted and enriched itself ever since.

The Syrian campaign had started. This was a sorting out of the Vichy French, who thought that to join the Free French was supporting a lost cause. As a small group of engineers, we were to make our way north towards Syria on the eastern side of Galilee, via Derra. I was in the CRE's staff car as we drew towards Derra. It was not certain that the "Vichy" had evacuated, so the Colonel turned to me and said, "Smith, is there anyone in this group you would like to come in? If we go in first there's always a chance that we might be in the 'bag'" (i.e. captured). I looked back and shouted, "Anyone been in the boy scouts?" If one was to spend the rest of the war in a compound then who better than an old scout could I choose for company. At least if we escaped we could survive, remembering the old days in the 7th Dover and all the fun we had on escape games. "Och aye!" came a voice from the back of our small convoy, and this

Nurse Joan Hemmingway of the Hatfield Spears Unit — 1942

commenced a long friendship. Staff Sergeant Robert T Sime from Rutherglen came into our car and the three of us made for the end of the escarpment approaching Derra. As we moved in the enemy moved out! They thought we were many more in number; they may even have thought we were slick fighting troops when in fact only three of us had had basic infantry training; the rest of our group were architects, engineers and technicians. We moved in and found an old building which offered at least shelter from the sun in the day and the cold at night. When Jock and I had found a corner on the "safe side" of the concrete house we looked around to find out about the town, if that is what it could be termed.

To our amazement we saw across the field a large marquee with a huge red cross painted on the side, and to add to the interest there were real NURSES going about their duties. This was it — we must organise a party and invite them over. The officers were in full agreement provided we did the work. A quick "shufti" in the village produced wine and titbits in exchange for English cigarettes. Somehow in such a situation soldiers can always turn up with the goods. Jock and I went over to the marquee and found the Matron, who said that they would like to come over and spend the evening with us, if only to catch up with UK news. They had been out in the Middle East much longer than any of us, and as they were the Hatfield Spears unit which consisted of a number of Quakers they were eager to hear from us. Our particular nursing friend was Sister Joan Hemmingway. She was not very tall but one of the most interesting personalities that one could ever meet. Apart from nursing, she could fly a plane, drive a heavy lorry, and converse with anybody about anything. I understand that she was related to Ernest Hemmingway the writer. She was also very beautiful, and the officers had their own ideas. She told them that she was invited by the Staff Sergeants and would spend the evening with them rather than take a ride in the jeep.

I went to Italy two years later, and who was it came to a party we arranged but Joan Hemmingway! I was by then an officer and so had access to a 15 cwt lorry; and she agreed to come and visit an old castle. On the way back the engine stopped. After I had made several unsuccessful attempts to get it going, Joan said, "Move over and let me try." In no time she had it going, and to my comment that I didn't think a woman could know that much about any army vehicle she replied, "This thing is like a Meccano — easy. You should see me fly a plane!" These nurses did so much beyond the call of duty. I recall when they went up into the hill in their leave time, through the snows, to care for civilians in the villages who were suffering through the war. True dedication is no doubt the willingness to serve and not to seek for reward or count the cost.

Let us move back to the Middle East again, and to the hills overlooked by Mount Hermon. Jock and I spent some time at Kunetra, a small township which seemed to have more mosques than houses. We found a hut in a large field, and our task was to prepare for the building and repair of a road, which since has seen the ravages of war several times. Every night the dogs from the hills would come down to the perimeter fence we had made for the safe-keeping of the lorries. One dog seemed to us very attractive. Could we charm it into being our guard dog? A chunk of meat on the end of a piece of string, shortened by stages each night, resulted in the dog, which we named Lassie, being our faithful pet. She slept in the hut with us and was awake at the slightest sound of prowlers from the village. They were soon off when Lassie barked. Our dog was happy with us, but the call of the wild and her pack became too strong. One day she took one long last look at us, howled, and ran away to join the pack. Jock and I formed a strong kinship there in the hills, as we talked about home and the things that matter. We knew that nearly two thousand years before, on much of the territory we worked on, Christ had carried out his ministry of healing and care.

Eventually we reached Damascus and were able to retrace the steps of St Paul down the street called Straight. There were no good guide books, so what better than the New Testament! The whole story came alive, and one of my treasured possessions is a tin of soil from Bethlehem. Can one get nearer to the Master?

Just a point, by the way. Recently I was invited to what was called the largest church in a certain area; it sat two thousand people. I found that the largest place of worship is the world itself — it "seats" millions and has within its boundless walls enough for everyone. I wish that it were shared, and then within its walls there would be no children starving. However, what I have just written has given me an idea for a Sunday sermon. Come along sometime and hear the rest of it.

We had been preparing for the building of a road. There is so much planning to be done before one bit of metalling is laid, and to learn the terrain in detail I was given a stretch of road from Asdot Yacoub (Jacobs Ladder) to Damas to repair. I had to recruit my own labour from the villages, and during our work we had to master the local Arabic the long way. You can get by with about two hundred words, and ample signs with the odd laugh. I set out lengths of the road, about three kilometres for a day's work. This was done by placing stones across the road. When the Arabs had done their stint they could go home. I noticed that each day they finished early, so to get value for money I extended the stint a hundred or so metres further. Still they finished early and it left me puzzled as they still had the same number of men working. I then met the village headman. Hassed was a picture book Arab; his horse, snow white, was a magnificent sight, and he in his flowing robe looked to me like Rudolf Valentino in The Sheik film. He told me how every night they moved the stones back to confuse me, but said that the work would be done without my trying to be so strict on the daily quota scheme. It was done on time and done well.

Hassed spoke perfect English and had the charm of a well educated Arab. He impressed me so much that I told my superiors about him. They too were of the opinion that it would be good for Anglo-Arab relations if he were to be given a commission in the Arab Legion. I lost track of him for a month or so, and one morning when I was measuring a section of the road I saw galloping across the desert my friend Hassed in the smart uniform of the Legion with the field rank of Major. I saluted smartly as he dismounted and came towards me. He just did not understand why I saluted him, and it took some explaining to assure him that it was his rank which required the compliment. But without a rank or smart uniform he was one whom I would salute anyway.

The road which was to result in my gaining a commission was from Merjaoun to the Damas-Beyrouth road junction — about sixty kilometres. It was to be a new road on virgin desert and hillside. Here and there we found tracks which were a good indication of the route we should take. After all, the mules which had been over that area for centuries were without any doubt the best recce surveyors. A mule will most certainly not work one bit harder than necessary, so the rule was to find the tracks and then link up with them. A rule we had in the Sappers was to exploit local resources in material and know how. I had to recruit about 2000 road workers who were to be employed by the Palestine Road Construction Company. This was under the control of Mr Perritz who taught me so much about the business. We took on whole villages, including children, the old, and even the infirm. There was something anyone could do, even if it was to carry a small basket of stones to the road line. The young women were the best workers as they were able to balance at least twenty eight pounds of broken basalt stone, in baskets, on their heads!! and walk with it to the most difficult places.

At first I did not like the idea of this, but had to submit to a deputation of really beautiful young women who said it was not fair if they could not do this heavy work. Who could find it in his heart to refuse them!

Certain rather specialist works were let out to Arab contractors, and it was at the bridge at Metulla on the Palestine/Lebanon border that I met an Arab whose traditional skill and technical knowledge amazed me. First the river had to be diverted so that the water course would be dry where the bridge was to be built. The timbering over which the stone masonry was to be set was mainly odds and ends of whatever wood was available. As a craftsman in wood, I could not have done it in the same way. I had to have proper scantlings cut carefully to size. It was by using advanced geometry that the mason cut out templates and profiles for the stones, which were being prepared by quite young children. The joints between the stones were barely 1/16th of an inch. When some hundreds of these stones were ready the whole bridge seemed to grow like a Lego set used by children in this country. The bridge with a span of 24 feet was perfect, and it had been built by — AN ARAB WOMAN! She told me that in her family, of which she was the last in a long line of masons, there were no men left. Her father had taught her the trade and her husband had been taught by her. She was the Master! and her man did what he was told, at least when they were at work. Their children also carried out the craft. Perhaps it was not so strange after all, because it is to the Arabs that the Western world owes many skills. If only men would appreciate that we all have so much to learn from each other, the world might be a happier place. When her bridge was complete I took Sariar to see a bridge that we had built. Ours was of reinforced concrete. She took one look at it and said "Mush Quoize." Translated into English this means, "What a load of rubbish."

My own small detachment of military personnel

Our Road in Syria — Lebanon 1942/43

A Road Culvert.

L/Cpl Cheek, Dvr Houghton, L/Cpl Clater (later Captain), Sgt Duncan, Jos, Cpl Moulding, Major Berks. D.C.R.E. (Roads)

Matulla Bridge — Sariah was the Mason!

consisted of a driver and a Sergeant, who was hoping eventually to go on a course for promotion to Clerk of Works. One day the Sergeant came into my tent, looking very glum. "Staff," he said, "I don't want to worry you too much but we have lost a steam roller!" Now, how on earth can anyone lose a thing like that? We had fifteen of them on the length of the road so there was always a chance that we had tucked one a way in a fig grove along the road, say at Kilo 12. This was a delightful spot where we often stopped for lunch. We took out the fifteen hundredweight to make a search. It was nowhere to be seen and we both became worried. In the end I decided that we would walk the length of the way and look in every possible spot. A high noon we stopped for our food in an attractive place. Standing on a high mound of rock which we have previously blasted from the hillside, I looked down into a ravine and there just protruding above the surface was the tell-tale wheel of our roller. Could we ever raise it? A further recce convinced me that where it had landed, when it rolled over the bank, was to be its last resting place — unless some enterprising Arabs salvaged it after the war. To finalise its loss we buried it by pushing one more rock over to cover it. It was eventually "written off" as unfit for further service. Indeed this was true, as from what we could see there was considerable damage done to it. I am convinced that in the Lebanon today there is a proud owner of a roller in some Arab village.

There is a place on the side of the road near Hasbani which is the source of the River Jordan. It is a huge lake caused by the melting snows of Mount Hermon which form springs bubbling up through the surface. On overflowing, the water forms a waterfall dropping into a pool some twenty feet below. It was in this part where the water was ice cold that we were tempted to swim. Nobody ever mentioned what other delights the water held. I soon found out and am sure that when I discovered what was there I broke the Olympic record for the crawl. Down the strip I swam quite happily until the Sergeant yelled out, "Get out, Smithy, there's a water snake nearly on you!" The pool was alive with these creatures and it was no time to investigate whether or not they were poisonous. Later we found out that they do make life unpleasant for those who dare to swim in their water.

At one stop on the road there were two Arab villages about half a mile from the way on either side of it. One afternoon while taking a siesta I was awakened by a runner who said that along the track there was a small war brewing up between the two villages, and that I must go along straight away and sort it out. What a tall order for one who had had no training in diplomatic dealings. Anyway, in for a penny, in for a pound. I decided to leave my revolver behind (it never did work, anyway) and became a trouble shooter. When I reached the huge angry crowd I found that two did speak a little English, so with my little Arabic, between us the grievance was made clear. The alignment of the road was such that one village was nearer to the road than the other, and for some reason best known to the contestants this gave an unfair advantage. The argument by the time I arrived had built up into an ugly situation, so something had to be done. The best way was to play it cool, so I lit my pipe and put to them my solution (with my own private prayer); "Give me one long-legged man from each village, let each walk back to the edge of his neighbour's village and with an escort to see fair play they will step out, counting the steps until they meet face to face. That then will enable us to decide a new centre point for the road." There was not much in it when we worked it out. Both villages thought that was a good idea and the whole situation was resolved. From their point of view justice was seen to be done as their long-legged emissaries paced it out. I was dined and wined with peanuts and arack — this being a transparent liquid which was meant to deceive Allah, who they said would be angry if they gave me red wine. The simplicity and shrewdness of the Arab was something to be admired and their generosity often taught me a lesson. If they had two and you had none they regarded it their duty to share, and you were obliged to accept.

In under a year the road was finished and I was told that Colonel Wavish was coming to inspect it. I was to be ready and properly dressed for this almost ceremonial occasion. The inspection party consisted of Colonel Wavish in the first car (me at his side whilst he drove), the contractor, and an amazing looking Arab in flowing robes. I had never seen him before but he did add a touch of colour to the tarmac and kerbstones. I had been warned that the Colonel had something important to say to me if he was satisfied with the work. We reached the end of the road and he turned to me, saying "Staff Sergeant Smith, if it is your wish I am prepared to recommend that you go forward for training at the Middle East OCTU, for (if you make the grade) a commission in the Royal Engineers. It will mean, of course, that you will have to write to me officially." "Thank you, Sir," I replied, "Here is the letter." I had written it the evening before. He looked a bit surprised and said, "Full marks for initiative, I'll take it from here."

I went back to the home of an Arab friend, Franka Burketa, a Christian, with whom I spent periods of rest leave during the building of the highway. I told him that in the near future I would be moving on for special training and possible promotion. He suggested that we visit the home of a Pastor Khuri in the village of Merjayoun. I took with me a Sergeant friend, Howard Bulpin. We were shown into the meeting room at the manse, where about twenty Lebanese Christians regularly met for their mid-week worship. It did strike us as strange that there were no women present, but in those situations it is better to keep a still tongue. In a little while in came the Pastor's daughter, carrying a huge brass bowl which had in it cold water from Hasbani. She quickly removed my army boots and washed my feet and those of my friend; she also washed everybody else's feet — it was cold. With all feet cleansed the Pastor said with almost a Papal authority, "You see, my friends, here we keep to that wonderful English tradition as did Jesus Christ." I became a bit mixed up at this point because I thought it was Christ who started it, not the English. We did not tell them that it was not a custom in England. Why spoil the delightful vision they had of life in the UK?

Clearing up after a large contract always takes time. It is called finalising and one has to sort out various claims, recover plant and machinery (if you haven't lost a steam roller along the road!), certify payments to sub-contractors, and a host of things which seem far removed from essentials in the winning of the war. All these duties had to be done whilst awaiting the result of my application for a commission.

I had some leave due and decided to visit Bethlehem. It was there that I had a moving experience. I walked to Bethlehem from Jerusalem and reached the Church of the Nativity where you have to bend down to enter the building — a good idea as it cuts you down to size right at the start of the visit. Many of us went in; there must have been about five different nationalities represented. Once in we were asked to buy long candles to light the way down the steps and into the grotto. This is a large cavern-like room and at one end, set into the wall, is a plaque, which bears the inscription, "HERE JESUS CHRIST WAS BORN." We stood there spell-bound or awestruck, call it what you like; but we were all very quiet — thinking — praying — recalling home — remembering Captain Stevens in my case, and my parents and Edith. In a sacred place all sorts of things pass through one's mind. A young Senegalese soldier stepped forward, knelt, and said the Lord's Prayer in his broken English. All of us present followed him in this prayer, and each in his own language. I am quite sure that God did not need an interpreter.

Indeed, one does not have to explain to the Almighty; our prayer has to be "Thy Will be done." Returning to Jerusalem we visited the Garden of Gethsemane and Golgatha. There one was mystified why people who worshipped the same god could blast each other to pieces. Perhaps when the war was over, I thought, all mankind would live together in the peace we had experienced in the grotto at Bethlehem. Let's get it over was the thought in many minds that day. If you, the reader, ever visit Jerusalem, do walk along the Via Dolorosa and capture the feeling of the place. Did I bring back any souvenirs? Yes, a little soil from Bethlehem. There's not much left now in my tin, as through the years I have sprinkled a little of it in various places where I have been invited to speak about some of my "chips on the floor."

It was soon after my visit to these sacred places that I was summoned to visit a Major General who had to give me the "once over" and say whether he agreed that I should go forward to the next stage in changing a carpenter and NCO into an officer. I was ushered into the ivory tower of the General who looked at the paperwork in front of him and said, "Hum...Hum (again), so you want to be a Sapper officer. What university did you go to?" This, I thought, was my lot — pack up your bags and get on to another road. I burned my boats: "HARDWORK, SIR." "Hardwork? never heard of it. Where is it? he asked. "In the workshops and on the building sites at home, Sir." This was chips for me, so I thought. He roared with laughter and said, "Staff Sergeant, that's the best bloody college of the lot. I'm sending you forward and the very best of luck to you."

I saw the same top brass over two years later and thought that he couldn't possibly remember me, a Lieutenant, and I edged away to talk with other Lieutenants in the club. He spotted me, came over and said, "Are you still in that college, Smith?"

For all soldiers there comes a time when they receive

marching orders. I was given seven days notice to report to the OCTU at Acre, and what a week this was to be! First, my NCO friends took me to Beyrouth for a party at the Top Hat Night Club on the seafront. It wasn't a disco — they hadn't been invented then — it was a jive session and a favourite spot for the Americans. Everybody joined in what was an all-the-evening jive. I was given, with her parents' permission, a young French lass, and believe it or not I found a new skill in the dance — if that is the way to describe it. She went over my shoulder, round in circles, got flung in the air, and generally I entered into the evening's fun. Why not? This was to be my last week as Staff. It was about one o'clock in the morning when an American came over and said, "Say, brother, I cede — you are the champ." I look back now and think — what are they all doing now, my mates? It comes to mind especially when at our Royal British Legion meetings we say the words of tribute — WE WILL REMEMBER THEM. Many of my friends did not, alas, grow old to see the going down of the sun and the early morning.

There were three days left before movement — how should these be spent? Christmas was near and I was not too far from my beloved Merjayoun where lived Franka and my Christian friends (Arabs). Howard Bulpin and I decided to hike from Nazareth over the hills towards Galilee and then north to Merj. Part of the way was covered by straddling a sack of grain in the motor sidecar of a Jewish lad from one of the settlements. What a sight it was to stand on the hills overlooking the Sea of Galilee and think that nearly two thousand years before another carpenter may have stood in the same place. I am sure that He did.

Very tired and footsore, we reached Merjayoun about nine o'clock in the morning. The reunion was wonderful and we were immediately invited to their little church to share in the Christmas worship. The Nativity was enacted by a local shepherd who brought his real sheep into the church, and to our surprise a three-day-old baby with his young mother were representing Mary and the Christ Child. Excuse me, reader, at this point. I have a lump in my throat and my eyes are running. Each to his or her tradition wherever they are in the world. We all have so much to learn from the land where it all started — the place where they have no tinsel or glass baubles, and where many refugees have so little to eat. Their only deep freeze may be frozen snow of Mount Hermon and the only sound that of gunfire and children crying.

When the Pastor took us to his home for a drink of goat's milk he gave the toast: "May you all return to your homes when the war is over, and often remember — US." With Christmas over we made our way back, to part our separate ways — Howard to his unit and I to the most strenuous training I have ever known.

Chapter 6

Reporting to a series of camps I arrived eventually with about seventy other cadets at the entrance gate to the OCTU training camp. The gate was closed and we waited until a Sergeant Major Gribble from New Zealand arrived. He took one look at us and actually screamed at us, "Good heavens, the war is as good as lost if you gentlemen are going to finish if off!" He looked to us at that stage as if he was going to be airborne at any moment. "While you are here you'll work so hard you will all wish that you had never been born. March at the double, report to the office and get settled in. You have forty minutes to be back on parade with full marching order. If by nine o'clock this evening anyone of you feels that he wishes to return to his unit, he is free to do so. Cadets!!! at the double — march!". One or two turned it in there and then. In forty minutes most of us were on the parade ground where we were drilled for an hour. On dismissal we were told to be in the lecture hall dressed in our best, complete with blanco-ed belts and white hat bands. What a scramble it was! As we filed into the hall who should I meet but my friend, Jock Sime. Neither of us knew at the time that each of us would be on the course. He was one month my senior, having started a month earlier. How useful this proved to be as Jock knew the "ropes of survival" at the camp.

Our day started at six in the morning with PE under the eye of an APTI, who knew just how far he could stretch us before we collapsed. We ran, jumped, swam, climbed ropes, and then slid down them upside down. It was very strenuous and each session lasted for forty-five minutes.

After PE we had to double back to our hut, clean it up, make our beds tidy to the prescribed pattern, dress in the order for the day, have breakfast, and be on the parade ground by 0800 hours. What a pace it was! There was more drill, followed by weapon training, lectures and schemes, notebooks to keep going — these were scrutinised every week and marked with many caustic comments. We had a party one evening when we were given a "free" — although it was still under the watchful eye of an instructor who would have no hesitation in reporting any conduct not in keeping with that of an officer and a gentlemen. Very late that night as we made our way back to the hut we saw a small palm tree growing not far from the Company Office. Every morning after PE the instructor would tell us to double round the tree and get ready for the next period of training. We decided to lift it and with ceremony replant it about half a mile further down the desert — that would sort out the PE staff. In the end the joke was on us because the next morning our instructor said his usual piece, "Double round the tree and away for the next session!!" This of course made us later for the chores in the hut. We could not bend the system in way, so late the next night the tree had to be replanted in its former position — this time without ceremony. It was long after we had left the OCTU that we found out that this escapade had become a tradition ever since the camp had been taken over for training purposes.

This course included unarmed combat and we were told by the Sergeant to take a dive at him (nothing barred). He would then throw us hard on the sand and show his delight at our inexperience. His great piece was to tell us he was going to attack us. He came like a bull and we felt worse than ever. But our day came when he flung himself at one of the lads who jumped lightly into the air. To our delight the Sergeant slid face down on the sand. He turned for a second fling and again the soldier moved — this time sideways and placed a foot neatly to one side, which caused an even better slide. For the first time the Sergeant had met his match and was not amused as he cleaned up his wounds. Our lad was a ballet dancer! I wonder if he ever used this skill against the real enemy in action? The moral of the story is — never under estimate the toughness of a ballet dancer if you are in a spot of bother at Sadlers Wells!

Jock and I on one occasion found ourselves together on a night scheme. These were quite fun because the staff chose a foggy evening on half moon. Each cadet had a turn at being a Commander and had to answer to the field officers as to how he was controlling his men. There seemed to be a magic phrase "two up, one back." This means that with three companies you could look after the left and right flanks with the HQ company back — and of course ready if they were needed. We moved in the night — crawling and damp — and couldn't see a thing. Then out of the gloom loomed a figure wearing a white armband. He said to Jock, "What is the disposition of your troops?" Jock looked up and replied, "Sorry Sir, not a clue." At least Jock was honest in his reply as none of us could see anything. He was relegated for one month and I made sure that when my turn came I would give the "two up, one back" answer. It seemed that if you knew these magic "Open Sesame" expressions then the wretched war could be won.

Next to me in the hut was an Aussie (Australian) Cadet West. Being the last all-Empire intake we were able to learn much about our friend from "down under." Edith and my mother used to save their ration of eggs and flour and make for me a cake as big as they could afford — generally five inches in diameter. It was a real sacrifice. They also put in the parcel a tin of Gold Block tobacco and some sweets. When the parcel arrived in the hut whoever was nearest to the door simply opened it, tossed over the tobacco and letter, then sliced up the cake so that we had a bit all round. Rough on me, but when the cakes arrived from "down under" the same rule applied — then we all had a very large slice because their cakes were enormous. We all learned the lesson of share alike, be it a lot or a little. Old "Westy" won the Allenby Sword for efficiency and he was truly proud of it. He was a sheep shearer by trade and used to say that it would take more than a war to take the wool off his back. I often wonder where he and the other lads are, and whether they have a thought of this writing "Pommy"?

Our passing out parade was indeed something we will always remember. It matched Sandhurst minus the white horse up the steps. There followed the parties and some occasional leave to call off following what was the finish for some, and half-way for those of us who were going on for specialist training in the technical corps. I made the grade for the infantry and was told that I was to go on to Ismalia to complete the training for a commission in the Royal Engineers. At this stage the reader can stand momentarily to attention or turn the sound off on the TV!

Jock had previously moved on to Ismalia and so was ahead of me. Again he knew the ropes and was able to tell me to acquire a second set of webbing. Without this one was lost as they had a wonderful way of seeing that we fell in the mud along the Nile bank and then demanding that we be back on parade in twenty minutes looking as if we were to mount guard outside Buckingham Palace. I thought about this when I went recently and saw the smartness of the Lifeguards inside the Palace.

Sapper training was quite different. Defusing bombs, laying and clearing minefields, building bridges, demolitions, boatmanship and map reading. So much to cram in in such a short time meant that we were to work even harder than at the Infantry School.

To avoid PE I opted to join the long-boat rowing team. After all, I came from Dover and surely this rowing would be easy. What they did not tell us was that the rowing was being supervised by a Cambridge Blue! Instead of starting at 6 a.m. he made the rowers get up at 5.30 to get the boat out and not lose a minute of good rowing time. Once in the longboat — an enormous craft — he picked me out for stroke oar. We were soon in the water and our coach mounted his cycle, adjusted his megaphone, and to his melodious intoning of, "In....Out....In....Out....," we began to pick up speed on the Suez Canal. Just as we were all beginning to enjoy it he quickened up the pace, "In..Out..In..Out.." and kept it that way until we were all ready to die. Then he slowed up a little to ease the pressure. That "Blue" knew exactly how far to stretch the crew. Day in and day out we were trained to handle the boat; eventually we manoeuvred it like a singles shell on the Thames at Richmond. None of us realised that we were being trained for the big race of the Staff versus the Cadets. The staff had never been beaten and the trophy was the golden oar. It was just an ordinary oar painted with gilt, but once we knew what was at stake our enthusiasm grew alarmingly. All our spare time was spent down at the boathouse training for the big event. By now you will have guessed that the cadets won. What a race it was, and few of us had any idea that all this hard work was not simply to win the golden oar but was preparation for our part in combined operations at a later date. I do hope that when we British pulled out of Egypt after the war the trophy found its way back to the RE Depot Museum at Chatham — 'cause it's got my name on it as stroke oar!!

Before we were given our results on the continuous assessment system used, we were called into the Commandant's office and asked a very important question. "If you are not sent to the Royal Engineers on being commissioned, what do you wish to do?" My reply was, "Join my father's regiment, the Queen's Own Royal West Kents." The Commandant then said, "And if not there — where?" My reply was "Wherever those with more experience than I have decided that I can best serve to finish the war off as soon as possible." This pleased him and he informed me that I had made the grade and was to be posted to a works unit as soon as it could be arranged. Both Jock and I made the grade, and although we were for some time separated we did eventually catch up with each other again back in the UK at Halifax — in the ablution house when we were waiting for a posting to Europe! So much time in the services seems to be spent waiting. I went to the Depot and waited — at Ismalia.

Almost as soon as we arrived at Ismalia we were briefed about the actual day of our commissioning. We were to be flown to Cairo to what was once King Farouk's Palace, and there at a special parade the seal of approval would be set. On March 11th seventy of us were formed up on the verandah and we wondered who the officer for the day would be. I cannot recall his name but he came out from the UK specially for the event. His speech was brief and to the point. "Gentlemen, you are now officers in your respective regiments. When you leave here you will undoubtedly make many mistakes. Remember this: determine to do your job with zest and enthusiasm. If you make a mistake make a big one, 'cause you will get into just as much trouble if you make a little one, and the chances are even that in the end it will not be an error that cannot be put right. Parade, dismiss." What could have been briefer than that, but I found on many occasions that the advice was sound — even in civilian life.

Back to the camp to await a posting. The days dragged on and to fill in the time we did the routine duties of young officers. Fire pickets, messing supervision, checking sick parades, and — my speciality — signing leave passes. How did one get out of this and find a unit where one could further the war effort? After two days I had it. Let 'em all go on leave. By the time I had signed enough passes almost to empty the depot the permanent staff officers descended on me with words to the effect that I was a menace to the depot and, to my delight, I must go. Within three days my posting came up. I was to report soonest to Palestine only a few miles from my road which had started it all off. However, "soonest" meant that I was to take a week's leave and fully kit myself with all the impedimenta that changes a Sergeant into an Officer. I was given £68 and a month's advance of pay — I believe it was about £20. What did one do with all this money and a seven-day pass? I teamed up with another young officer and we decided to take a trip to the upper Nile, to the regions of Luxor and Kanark. Our cash stretched to staying in the Winter Palace Hotel at Luxor. In peace time it was used by millionaires and Princes, and were we two Second Lieutenants going to live up it up! At the "Palace" we quickly settled into the comforts of air conditioning, complete with an Arab whose task it was to see that our every need was supplied. As we were enjoying a drink he came in and with great ceremony said, "Gentlemen, your wish is my command. Whatever you desire I will arrange," and he bowed. (Good heavens, I thought, I'm really a carpenter. What is happening to me? It cannot be real!). My response to his announcement was more in fun than a serious request. "Ahmed, this evening we shall like to sail down your beautiful Nile in a falouker with a man playing violin music to us — and two English nursing sisters as our guests." He went off and we thought no more of this until at ten o'clock that night Ahmed returned, bowed, and proudly announced that our wishes had been prepared — all was ready for our pleasure. We were almost scared stiff, but in for a penny or a pound, it was all there as we requested. The nurses were staying at the hotel nearby and Ahmed had approached them with the same Middle East flair. Can you imagine us in the middle of a war enjoying such delights — it was good fun and the nurses were good sports. Our party of four visited all the ancient places in Luxor, and never will I forget Tutankhamen's tomb in the Valley of the Kings. We were spellbound and enthralled by the wonder of it all. We were told all the stories about the curses which befell those who entered the tombs in the days of the Carter expeditions in Egypt. Later in Alex I tracked down a medical man who was with Carter at the time of the discoveries and he said that the men would not rest in the noon day heat. He warned them about heat exhaustion and the collapse which might follow. I mentioned the curse stories and he just smiled. "Take my advice," he said, "When in Egypt take a rest in the high noon, if you want to go on living." Our week went all too quickly and we made our way back to Cairo — broke — with all sorts of gear to buy. Some urgent thinking needed to be done or we were in trouble.

In the main street of Cairo I noticed a branch of Overseas Barclays and wondered whether there was an opportunity there of doing business. We went in, only to be met by the manager who said that, to the best of his information, we were the last of the subaltern intake which he felt sure would be in to see him. To our surprise we found in the room most of our friends were there, and equally broke. The manager gave us a friendly lecture about being thrifty and then announced that he would help us by a loan of £60, plus enough to see us through until the next pay advance. He made it quite clear that if we did not already have an account with Barclays in the UK, this was the time to settle. Most of us did, and I am sure that many of Barclay's older customers made their first contacts with the bank during those difficult days. With the cash advanced we soon bought all that we needed and went our different ways to the units detailed.

This very nervous Second Lieutenant found his unit not far from Tyre and Sidon. Walking into the mess I saw the CO sitting back enjoying his afternoon "snifta." I saluted and announced my name, "Second Lieutenant J J Smith, Sir, reporting for duty." "Come in, sit down and tell me all about yourself — and, what are you drinking." "If it's all the same, Sir, may I have an orange — at least before sundown." He seemed satisfied with this and then looked as if he was ready for the rest of my history. I told him that by trade I was a carpenter and joiner and that seemed to be all that he wanted to know because at that point he said I was to take over the workshop side of the Company and produce for him a well-made travelling box. He had in mind, I found out later, the move of the Company to new operations in the Middle East. We had in the area nearby a mountain of timber which had to be graded and marked with a weird and wonderful system of coding — it eventually was landed in Italy and became bridges and huts for the troops in that campaign.

I had the usual routine duties of an officer, and one which I did not enjoy was the censoring of mail. In one letter was a photograph of one of the boys who had signed it and added the comment, "I can't tell you where we are, Mum, but I'm OK." This was quite in order and I duly stamped it for the post. There appeared many other similar photos and it struck me that something was not quite right. They were all taken near to a cement factory at Chekka and all of them were in a slightly different position, showing just one letter of the name of the factory. From a careful positioning of all the photos on the table I was able to see that the photographer could have produced from his negatives a good photo of the whole area, including the name, CHEKKA CEMENT FACTORY — LEBANON, and by blowing up the side views of the soldiers their regimental identification was easily established. We could not locate the photographer or even stop their transmission to — who knows? Production from the factory was entirely for the war effort and something had to be done before it became a target for an enemy raid. We made a mock-up of the factory further down the coast and arranged for a camouflage of our own. The mock-up did suffer a raid and no one was injured in our area. So much of the war was a matching of wit against wit, and we didn't always win. In addition to the workshops, I was given the cement works to supervise. How thankful I was for the days of learning about cement at the Dover Tech years before. It was a good job that the works had experts who knew far more than I did about their product. Being near to Tyre and Sidon where ships were made (as they had been made for centuries) entirely in wood, we also took over shipbuilding so that our cement could be sent to various places undetected by enemy radar. One of the shipbuilders with whom I became friendly let me have a go at shaping the bow of one craft, using a adze — a cross between a pickaxe and an oversize chisel — and to set off the experience you had almost to stand on your head and watch that you didn't cut your feet off. To so many of the natives I met, the fact that this young officer was a carpenter was a novelty. I was invited to their homes and when it came to the exercise of public relations I was "home and dry." To win the respect of the arab you must be able to do something which is practical. Their idea of an officer is one who can only tell another what to do, and be unable actually to do it.

In our unit was Captain Lou Kent, the author of books on practical mechanics and engineering. He was so helpful to me and spent many hours explaining the mysteries of engineering by using forks and knives balanced on cups at the most extraordinary angles. He made the whole subject come alive and at the end of my association with him I was beginning to be the embryo of an engineer. Needless to say, after the war it was the Kent & Reynolds books I used in lecturing. I only hope I made things as clear as Lou did in the Lebanon.

As was the custom, when we were almost enjoying the place and our work, our movement orders came — this time to Egypt in preparation for the Italian Campaign. In advance the CO, Major H J A Brown had to go to Egypt first. I had to go with him by car across the Sinai Desert. The Adjutant, Captain Hatt, chose me because as he said if we got stuck in the sand my prayers might get us out. One's commitment to Christianity was always respected in the army. Often they would "pull a leg" but somehow leaned upon one when there was stress. Our drive across the desert was uneventful except for the engine boiling up and a parley with some Bedouins we met on the way. Some of them did not realise there was a war on, or if they did they were cautious enough not to tell us. I told them that our problem was the constant boiling up of the engine and they solved the situation — keep a reserve supply in a goatskin hanging over the side of the car. The chief explained that when there was evaporation there was bound to be a drop in the temperature. Further talk revealed that he had been to a Western University! Why was he in the desert? "Allah gives space here and sufficient for our needs." Desert wisdom.

It was in the desert that I saw my first mirage — a boat in the sky and sailing upside down!! Were we mad or were we near some place? We were — it was the Suez Canal. These psychical wonders must be seen to be believed. Not until the end of the journey did one think back and realise that our trip could have gone wrong and these horrible vultures which can be seen in the air might have finished us up as food.

In due course the rest of the Company joined us at Alexandria and for a few weeks we enjoyed Egypt, visiting the Pyramids at Geza, the museums, and some wonderful swimming in the Meddi. Again, when we all thought that this was an ideal life for soldiering we were quickly given our orders for embarkation. None of us knew much about what was going on — why should we? Take it as it comes always seemed to be wiser. The ship moved from Alex in the middle of the night, and when we woke up in the morning we were well out at sea, out of sight of land. Destination? We all had a pretty good idea, but one could never be sure. Enjoy it while you can is always the best way of looking at the situation. In war you can be blown to pieces at any time, and then it's all over.

I always carried a very small compass, about two

centimetres in diameter. With it I found that our average course was north west, and this meant Italy. I was not far out because one morning we were in sight of that lovely island Sicily. There was the sound of gunfire on the shore and we found out later that the enemy was pulling out in haste. The Allied soldiers who had arrived before us were advancing, and this made our landing more like a day trip from Dover to Calais in peacetime. Amid the noise we had a good look round and several of us found an English church in the main street of Syracuse. We went in, and sitting next to me was a lady in a khaki uniform which was a little different from that worn by nurses and ATS. At the end of the worship I found that she was a member of the Salvation Army. For something to say I said that it was a long way for her to come — would she be returning with us to base? She replied, "Base? Oh no, I'm going forward to where the battle is; there may be lads there that need us." Isn't there a hymn which has something to say about "where duty calls or danger be never wanting there"?

An observation by the writer: in our many traditions within the Christian Church there are those who "preach and don't" whilst the Sally Army "preaches and does." I do hope our little salvationist came through the war safely. Even if she didn't her spirit lives in the world today.

It took a week or two to organise our workshops and plan our future of follow-up work in the Italian campaign. When all was ready for what we hoped might be a long stay in this delightful island more movement orders came through and we were told to pack up all the gear and be ready for a move. In very little time we had de-shipped our gear and reloaded it on another, but we were to travel by a landing craft. These rather peculiar boats were unprovided with cabins or any sort of luxury: you found a corner and made the best of it. The Captain had been unable to sleep for days on end and was almost "all-in". Major Brown and I suggested to him that perhaps we might help by "driving" the boat if he told us what to do.

81

We convinced him that if we were all to reach our destination in one piece he should get some "shut eye". He briefed us in the arts of seamanship — keep the boat on a course so that the compass needle kept on a certain bearing (I forget what it was), and if it appeared to vary I was to speak up the tube to the Major who would then adjust the wheel to correct the boat. It all sounded very simple and off we went. In the night the Major called down the tube and said there was a lot of old oil drums around the ship — what to do? "Go straight on," I said, "If it is a wreck or something, have a look for survivors and I'll call the Captain." Some hours later the Captain appeared looking a little refreshed and asked if there had been any incidents. I told him about the drums.

"What action did you take?"

"Drove straight on."

"Heavens, man, that was a minefield!" (I felt sick at this stage).

"Well, thank the Lord that you were in the wheelhouse. I should have taken evasive action and none of us might have been here this morning — no self-respecting enemy would think that any idiot would go straight through that lot!"

I did thank the Lord, and was pleased that I had joined the Sappers instead of the Royal Navy. I am quite sure that they would not have had me anyway. I never would have mastered all the wonders of port and starboard, fore and aft, not to mention all the fantastic technology of the sea.

Taranto was our destination on the mainland of Italy. Again there was sound of gunfire as we came into the port. It seemed to us an atmosphere of the unusual. The CO said that as I had infantry training I was to take a party to recce the landing situation (Why me I thought?) Anyway, with four of the lads we made our way to the dock gates stealthily. I had to lead the small party. The gates were open; were they boobytrapped? check them out — OK.

Watch those buildings over there — a movement by that doorway across the street — gates OK. A figure emerged from the doorway and came towards me. He was an Italian carrying a tray, and as he drew close he said, "Ice-creamo — very cheapa." What a relief! We found out from this man that the Germans had pulled out a few hours before our arrival, so we had Taranto to ourselves.

Orders came that our CO was to fly to Naples, together with the adjutant and one technical officer. That was three away, and at that stage it left a Lieutenant "Pancake" Smith and myself in charge of the machinery, and about 50 NCOs and men. The retreating Germans ahead of us had finished up in the bag so we had a fairly easy run up towards Naples. We were welcomed by most of the villages en route, and frequent checking of the roads for mines meant that all the training, even in the art of "delousing", paid off. We reached Naples, and for the first time felt that there we were likely to stay put for some time. The enemy was well north of us, although from time to time they did liven things up with raids on the city. I requisitioned a technical college workshop, well-equipped with woodworking and metal machinery. As workshops officer I felt very much like a principal in a college at home. My foreman was a civilian named Panicci and one of the best Italian craftsman I ever met. He could never understand how it was that a British Army Officer was able to show him how to produce from wood something uncommon to the Italian woodworker. To him all officers were rather helpless in matters practical.

It was not long before our unit took the shape of a borough engineer's works depot, something like those at home — or what we could remember of them, because we had been so long away from England that even names in the streets of or home towns were beginning to grow dim in the memory. Our unit rebuilt the essentials of the city in respect of water supply, drainage and electricity. If any of the readers of this little book think that the army cannot do any civvy job, then think again! The Royal Engineers have somewhere done 'em all. Let's name a few — Docks operating, railways, bridging, roads, electrical and mechanical workshops, water supply, drainage, hospitals (including the care of the nurses!). One of my most exciting memories is that of forestry — going out into the mountains to get logs for the saw mills at the foot of Mount Etna in Sicily. The Corps gives an opportunity for experience in so many different fields — just imagine being substitute for a Padre on the side of Mount Hermon in Syria and taking a church parade — all six of us!

In my office in Naples our cleaner, Maria (they were all called that name), every morning placed a vase of fresh roses on my table next to the photograph of Edith. I thought that Maria must be spending a lot of her own money, so I mentioned to her that she really shouldn't be doing all this for me in such austere times. She said that the people from whom she "nicked" them would never know — they got up too late in the morning — and she felt it was important to give me a daily reminder of home. She was a good soul, Maria.

The appalling poverty of Naples in the war years I will always remember. Often we would give the contents of our waste food bin to the locals for their "pet dogs", knowing full well that the dog would only get a share after they had found a few bits which they could eat. We were occupation troops in a beaten country which had become the pawn of Facism.

What a delight it was to learn that our nursing friends from the Syrian days were in Naples at the 65th General Hospital. More parties and outings — in between the raids which were now less frequent. All this was too good to be true, so we were again moved on to more active situations further north. No longer did we build bridges from wood, or lay motor tracks in old railway sleepers. We became all "mod". It was Bailey Bridges and Sommerfield Track. The tide of war had turned, and what good news it was when one day we were given a special contract: to rebuild and make operational a — wait for it! — BREWERY!!!! I'll always remember the CO when he pointed to me and said, "Hey, Joe, it's your job — you don't drink much and there will be more for us when you've finished it."

On the day that we heard the news of Italy surrendering I saw two Italian boys just outside our camp perimeter fighting with knives for the scraps out of the mess tins which soldiers emptied over the fence. We had them in and fed them. Strictly irregular, but what else could we do? The man of men once said, "Feed My flock".

There was so much that happened in those days. Much of it is recorded in work by other writers; the criticisms, condemnations — and much which to me still has security value. Let's keep it that way.

Many of my friends and I were involved in clearing up the mess that war leaves behind it. Some of my fellow officers and men with whom I worked were sent back to the UK, and then on to Europe from which they did not return. We shall remember them.

I was posted back to Sicily to organise rest hotels and hospitals. This truly was a soft number and far removed from the hazards of what was left of the war — the bloody onslaught of beating the enemy on his own ground. Maybe some ordinary fellow will write up this story. Just a minute, Spike Milligan has already done this if you would like to read his account.

The warmth of Sicily and the music in the cafés, the friendliness of the folk, all added to my own personal "run down." There one could catch up with letter writing and begin to feel a return to some sort of normality.

Out of the blue one day came a letter from my old Principal, Mr Jacques, who told me that he had kept tabs on me over the years, and now that the war looked as it it was slowly coming to an end he had it in mind to obtain for me an early release, if it was my wish. He invited me to join his staff as a lecturer in building subjects. What an opportunity this was, and to think that the Principal who had done so much for me recalled the days when he intimated that one day I might be on his staff. This was on the very day when my father took me to the tech to make a start on further education in building. The wheels started turning to change this officer of the Royal Engineers back into a civilian — not as a carpenter but as a lecturer in the subject which had been first taught by Bill Wood and my early mates. I returned home to the UK thinking that it was all to be straightforward — home, then out. It was not to be because the army had other ideas. The experience I had gained in the overseas theatre of war meant that they wanted me in Europe to help out with the smashed up towns of Germany. Oh Eck! was my first reaction, and indeed Edith was equally disturbed as we had been separated for so long. Edith wrote to Winston Churchill (I didn't know) and believe it or not she had a reply signed by the great man himself. In it he said that I was needed — me! just an ordinary chippy. After a short leave I was once more on the move, this time to Halifax to await a posting to Germany. How silly to go to Halifax when Germany is not all that distance away from Dover!

As an old hand I found that the young officers I met were so interested in what I had seen, and the common question was, "What's it like over there?" One morning I went to the ablutions and next to me, to my utter surprise, was my old friend, Jock. We were both equally amazed that again our tracks had met. We were both destined for Germany and it was a wonderful opportunity to catch up with all the news. Knowing that we might be going to Europe via Dover, we planned somehow to get off the train at that town and spend an hour with Edith and my parents. We "squared" the RTO to send for us at Dover; he said that we might have just two hours off the train; then a telegram to Edith, "Jock and I home for an hour — just a cuppa", and as soon as the train pulled into the station at Kearsney Halt we were off in a taxi to Maxton.

My folk had prepared a meal from their meagre rations — bacon, eggs and all the tea we could manage. Every time Jock and I meet we recall the wonderful "hop off" the train.

Time passed all too quickly, and we were on our way to Germany — not very willingly, but after all "orders is orders". Our station was Badounhausen — not a bad place in those days but rubble everywhere and, I thought, a sense of bewilderment in the population. Everything about the army was different. Ones colleagues in the mess seemed to resent us old hands in a peculiar sort of way; there were far more parades and "BULL". Most of our colleagues spoke some German. I flatly refused to attempt it. If the Germans wished to contact me then they could ------ well learn English! Not a very Christian attitude to take (I can hear some good folk saying it, and they are right), but I believe that we are forgiven our shortcomings, and even now the writer claims to be a struggling Christian. If ever you find it easy then think about it; there's something wrong if you find it easy.

Only one thing did I enjoy in Germany — joining the Montgomery choir of one hundred service people. We only did one piece which was Tales of the Vienna Woods. After the audition the choirmaster stood between two very large regular army Sergeants who really could sing. If I went wrong their glare was enough to put anyone right. Just after the grand concert which we gave to brighten up the depressed population and show them that as well as winning a war we could sing — my final orders came which granted a Class "B" release from military service. Mr Jacques had succeeded in convincing the War Department that I would be better out than in. So off to York for my demob' — my last movement in uniform (although later on I did join the Home Guard when it was formed on the occasion of the Berlin Airlift).

At York — in at one end of the long hall as a Lieutenant and out at the other dressed as a civvy. Me in a trilby hat, new suit and an overcoat, after riding a mule in Syria dressed in a sheepskin coat and wearing an Arab headgear. No more drinking coffee with my friends the Arabs or diving into the pool of Dan in the Holy Land! but some part of me remained in the Jordan and in the Grotto at Bethlehem. Always remember, Christians in England, your faith started there and came to us; we did not send it to them. And if you've any colour prejudice, take note that Jesus Christ, the Saviour of mankind was Himself coloured.

I boarded the train at York for home, and — you won't believe it — I felt a little sad and inadequate. This was not the same person in many ways who joined up as a volunteer in 1940. All my wonderings were how, after so long apart, Edith and I would meet the changed situation and really start a married life. She too was a lot older, so we were at level pegging. This is just about the right place to close this chapter and move on to the post-war days of this ordinary fellow.

Chapter 7

In most memoirs written by famous people their story ends when the writer has either resigned from office, got the sack, served a term, or retired to the country to live in a farmhouse. This writer now commenced a new phase in his life, so if you the reader like to consider this as a kind of commercial break and slip out to make a cup of tea, take as long as you wish — there's no hurry.

Edith and I bought an old banger. It was a Standard and was good enough until my new Morris Eight was delivered. We had a wonderful holiday visiting old friends and "rewinning" the war as we shared experiences of the Battle of Britain, and my adventures in the Middle East. During the holiday I was also able to help father-in-law with his book keeping. How I remember the journey to London in our car. The traffic peers had really gone to town in painting white lines on the roads and putting down signs like turn left, turn right, straight ahead, no entry, keep in lane, and so on. We crossed London Bridge, moved alongside the Thames, then over another bridge, turned left and kept going until Edith said, "Do we have to keep going over London Bridge?" And then, at a most inopportune time, the "big end" went! The noise was alarming and reminded me of some of the noises associated with an advance of military heavy gear. Stuck between two London buses, I had to face a verbal storm from one of the drivers, who wound down his window and shouted, "It's alright now, mate, the bloody war is over!" We were indeed home in England.

With the holiday over and the official pay drying up, I had to do something about getting a job. The Principal,

Mr Jacques, had got me back but it was to be about a year before I could take up full-time teaching, due to all the problems of establishment and County Council approval. I thought the Army took its time, but one year in civvy street — it was a bit much.

My old governor, Fred Dolbear, invited me to join him as works manager for a spell, and his co-operation proved to be most valuable while I waited for my future to be sorted out. He knew all about my intention to become a lecturer at the local college. He found my experience in CRE works services to be an asset in the post-war development of his business. To assist me he was able, by an arrangement between himself and the local council, to release me to serve for a time as Clerk of Works. These immediate post-war days were difficult for all sections of the construction industry, and often there was an arranged lending of personnel. To me it was like being posted in the army. I did some evening teaching at the Tech; this no doubt was to give the authorities an opportunity of judging whether I could do the job before appointing me full-time.

We soon became part of our old church in the High Street, and as this had suffered badly from bombing (it was almost a wreck) we met in the Town Hall for Sunday services. We used the Maison Dieu Hall which all round the walls had an assortment of armour, flags and pikestaffs. We once sang that well-known hymn, "Rise up O men of God and put your armour on", and indeed there was enough on the walls almost to kit out a sapper detachment. I had a share in recovering what we could of the church, and that, together with lay-preaching and a busy time at my job, kept my hands full in resuming the role of civvy in a post-war Britain. In September 1947 I took up my post at the Technical Institute — they renamed it "College" later on. It didn't make any real difference but the authorities thought it sounded "posher!" Silly, isn't it, 'cause a bucket's a bucket whatever you call it.

My work was to teach a group of part-time day release apprentices the trade of carpentry and joinery, and as I moved around the workshop it took me in mind right back to the workshop in Naples, with Panicci and my Italian friends. Gradually other subjects were given to me and I found that teaching was something so very worthwhile and had opportunities I never dreamed of. Through the course of a week the students ranged from older men who like me had returned from the war to pick up the loose ends, to young lads who had their world before them. Their course was carefully monitored by a panel of local builders under the chairmanship of Mr Barwick. He was the principal builder in Dover and made a very big contribution to education at all levels in the area. We had the traditional Open Day when parents could come along to see the work of their offspring. Studies were in line with the requirements of the City and Guilds of London Institute for the many trades. Great stress was given to the practical side of the trades, and indeed if one had a City and Guilds certificate it was taken for granted that you were good. There were also opportunities to take the Associateship Examination of the Carpenters Institute. The craftsman was beginning to be recognised as a person worthy of demanding respect in society. Many of my early students are now teaching or holding lectureships in Polytechnics. I found a book in W H Smith & Sons in which there was an acknowledgement to a J J Smith of Dover Tech for his interest in the student work of the author many years before.

It was a big step forward when the Tech started its National Certificate courses in building construction. In these our more academic students were able to embark on more advanced studies and progress towards even greater heights in the business. Then there were the prize days, when some important person came down from London to make a speech and present the awards of books and certificates. It still puzzles me why important people always seem to come from London — unless a prophet is without honour in his own country! Those whom I enjoyed teaching most were the lads who had difficulty in learning; they were of that group which in some cases had been evacuated and whose education had suffered disruption. For example, one lad went to three different schools and at each one arrived when they were learning how to multiply in decimals. He missed out on division and consequently was an expert on one thing only, multiplication! In any case, how could a youngster properly concentrate on school when the country was at war. I moved away from the more academic to the problem which today has been given its special name — REMEDIAL. After eight years at the college I decided to enter the Secondary Modern area of teaching, and looked around for a school seeking such a teacher. Barton Road, Dover, had a vacancy which looked promising, so I applied and was appointed.

What a change this was from the world of the older pupil! I had to find some more adult student contact in order to preserve my sanity. The children were like any other children, my colleagues were good, but the "one in authority" as he described himself at one assembly, in the end caused me to walk out of the school and go fishing on the pier.

I had heard that there was to be a prison at Dover in the Citadel Barracks on the cliff top overlooking Shakespeare Beach. They needed a teacher and this offered what I was looking for — a teaching situation with adults whose need was special. ANY NAMES OR DETAILS FROM NOW ON in this writing about chips in the "nick" are fictitious, as I have a great respect for the Official Secrets Act, which I signed before being involved at the prison, and also because one must think of the feelings of those who are now out.

It was the first time I had ever been to a prison and I kept an appointment with the Governor, Major Miller.

He was and still is a tall, shrewd gentleman, who as well as being a disciplinarian has the right sort of compassion for winning the affection of staff and detainees alike. He wanted me to set up the woodwork area from scratch, and that meant that there was nothing to start with but a large room and a pile of joists and floor boards. Benches had to be made and also cupboards for the very few tools available. Allocated to me were four "trusties" — Darky, Tich, Smudge and 'Arry. Why they were in prison was not my business, and if they wanted to talk about it then there was no reason why I should not listen. I found that they spent some time "sounding me out" to see if I would become a carrier and if they could use me as a postman. To tempt one they would complain about the prison soap, which was carbolic, and say how they wished they could get hold of some Lux toilet variety. When the conversation moved into the "would it be possible for you to" stage, I referred them to the black book of regulations which every teacher had on entering the service. They knew the rules but "tried it on." Soon they realised that this teacher was not going to be an easy touch and finalised the "try on" in this way: "Mr Smiff, you know that black book you've got? Is it with you now?" "Why, sure, I always carry it with me." "Get a bradawl, make a little hole in the corner, and stick in on the ---- house wall!" They appreciated that there was no point in pushing their luck. I knew I was accepted by them and that we could get on with the job of making our workroom. Darky was a bricklayer by trade and one day told me that any self-respecting prisoner could get out of the place quite easily 'cause the bars in the toilet were inset badly — "A couple of good shakes and they'd fall out." It seemed that he was right and after consultation he was allowed to reset the bars to real security. Strange though it seems, the prisoner likes some form of challenge. If it's too easy to get out he doesn't want to know, make it difficult and he is prepared to try. The reaction of those in confinement is worth studying. This showed itself in our music room; the teacher would bring in classical music albums and the cons would sit in a large circle to listen. In the group I saw some real old lags, bent buckled and bashed, gently waving their arms to the charm of the music; so often they were dreaming of the world which they had opted to leave. I say opted, because after all in our country it's easy to keep out of prison. Live under the law and "keep your nose clean."

We took a few weeks to make our room into a workplace complete with benches, and the authorities provided us with a kit of tools and new wood for the classes. The object of the work was to rehabilitate the prisoner by an appreciation of being able to do something and enjoying it. The workshop itself was a good start in this direction and my four "trusties" thought it would be a good idea to form a woodwork club. We did not after all form such a club as the students were frequently being moved in those days, and as a corrective training establishment their next move was generally — OUT. If we succeeded in forming a right relationship then we had not failed. One thing always amused me. The eduction side of the prison came for admin purposes under the local education department and we had a normal class register like the one I had used in the tech. Each class was called name after name and the usual tick entered against each "student." There was never anyone absent!!! Only on one occasion was one missing and then the balloon well and truly went up. All had to return to their dormitories and the teachers were directed to a room, where for some time we felt like prisoners ourselves.

So often the media wrongly describe prison officers as being extremely hard and often crude. I challenge this because in my experience over four years I found that while there were some who had much to learn about human relationships, in the main the officers were sound in their dealings with the convicts. Two I will mention their real names because they had the respect of everyone in the nick. CPO Goodchild is now I am sure retired. One evening he came into our room on his round and we noticed that his uniform was wringing wet. One of the lads asked him if it was raining outside and he replied that it was a little wet where he had been. We thought no more of it until, on looking out of the window, we noticed that it was a wonderfully clear night, not a cloud to be seen. When the local newspaper came out on the following Friday there was a headline: UNKNOWN RESCUER SAVES YACHTSMAN. It described how a sailor had been saved by a uniformed person who quickly disappeared after the rescue. It was Mr Goodchild. Often he brought his dog into the workroom, and no doubt elsewhere; this was not to scare the lads but to let them make a fuss of his old friend. He was a man we all respected.

PO "Lofty" Smith was another who was fair in all his dealings. He knew of the personal problems and worries of many of the prisoners and was ready to listen. Not that he could do much because the service has its experts in matters of welfare. How often the ear of Lofty did much to ease the mind of a worried prisoner by simply listening!

I was invited once to attend the Sunday morning church service held in the prison chapel. Of course I accepted and, not wearing my best suit, arrived at the prison on the morning in question. Almost as if I was not known I was escorted to the chapel and offered an armchair at the rear of the building. There was quite a problem when I declined the armchair and said that I preferred to sit on the benches with the lads. After all, why should anyone have a special seat in the presence of God. I sat next to Tich and enjoyed the morning worship. That was the only invitation I ever had. Perhaps in the prison service the rule is "Sinners to the front and Saints to the rear." Whatever way it is, I am fairly sure that there are no special seats up there, or out there, whichever way you like to think about it. One thing I knew was that my rule book was inviolate and that relationship was established. I overheard one prisoner say to another, "Smiffy ain't a bad ole cock." Praise indeed.

As the work in the "nick" developed and we needed specialist tools (which although on order had not arrived), I was given permission to take along my own tools provided that I took them away after the class had finished. It was one evening after the class that I was going on to the Methodist Church in the town to talk to the young people at the Bible class. In my tool bag I placed my Bible in with the tools for convenience of carrying. Half way through the evening I wanted a special bradawl and called out to "Shirty" who was a not too bright convict, "Shirty, find an awl in my bag, please; I've got an awkward corner here and can't get over to my bag." Shirty opened the bag and made a quick mental note of everything inside. He found the awl and at the same time spotted the Bible. He picked it up and said, "That's a bloody funny place to keep a Bible, ain't it, guv?" Often the right things to say are given to us as pennies from heaven, and this was one of them. "Not so strange, Shirty, remember it all started in the carpenter's shop in Nazareth." For a long time that evening Shirty said nothing; it was as if he was mulling it over in his mind. Then almost an hour later he said, "Guv, you're right 'cause the Parson said He was a carpenter."

As our evening activities finished at eight o'clock I was often able to cram in something else after class. A memorable time was when the local flower show was being held in the Town Hall. I left the nick a little after eight, and not dressed up in my best suit (you were wise to look a bit rough when in the nick) went to the Town Hall, where there was a long queue paying to get in. I had no money with me 'cause if you've got any sense you don't take money inside. I knew the young lady at the ticket office and said, "Sorry, Jackie, I've got no money on me — I've only just come out of prison." That was it!! In front of me the queue suddenly moved forward and behind me the tail-end of the queue moved back — I was in the middle alone! I knew that in the nick there is always that rather nasty BO smell but I was sure I had not brought it out with me. As I moved around the inside the crowded hall I noticed that when I moved to one stand everyone moved to another. There are many morals to this story. You sort them out, and all I shall say is, "If you want to see a flower show get a job in prison."

Our Governor gave us permission to be letter-writers for prisoners who were unable to do this and sought our help. To be unable to write a letter home is tough, and one is trusted if invited by a convict to write for him. Nibbo asked me to write a letter for him to his wife, and we sat down in the corner for privacy as he had to dictate the letter. The opening went like this: "No. 974562398765. Dear Bag," at this point I said, "Surely she has a name you could use?" He replied, "Oh yes, but if I called her anything else but BAG she would think I didn't love her any more." If ever dear Bag reads this work she should be assured that Nibbo has some wonderful qualities and although he missed out on some along the way his virtues outnumber his vices.

Governor Miller told us every year that the margin between right and wrong or them and us is very narrow. Someone else said, "Judge not, lest thou be judged."*

Let me tell you the story of Izzy, a Jewish lad for whom life all seemed a bit of a mystery. He knew that I was a struggling Christian and on several occasions asked me questions like; What is the difference between the Salvation Army and the Church Army — why are these two regiments — why does the prison chaplain wear white when he preaches on Sundays and a sports coat on Monday? Every week there was a fresh question until the big one came "Mr Smith, who was this Jesus Christ feller

---

* Read "Inside Outside", a book by Major A Miller

and what did He do?" I explained to him as far as I was able to basics of the faith and told him that at Easter Christians remembered the crucifixion and on the third day the glorious resurrection. I wondered what his reaction would be. I was amazed and taught something that I will always remember. I'll have to give it to you with language complete.

"After all that He did for the Jews what a bloody rotten lot we were to nail him up. You say that He accepted all that stick and didn't appeal?" I listened on — "Didn't anyone take His case up? He could have got off with a year in the Scrubs." It then dawned on me, the lad was bringing the story right up to the present day. The justice that he saw around him was in his mind recrucifying Christ every day of the present age. The lesson? Perhaps he was right and that so many of us think only in terms of two thousand years ago. I had not studied theology in any depth up to that time. I've read quite a lot since and am still only a very ordinary person who doesn't know all the answers, but I'll always thank God for putting Izzy in my way.

Another lad wanted to take an external examination in mathematics. As he was allowed to work at his sums instead of doing more heavy tasks he kept us going with all the marking and correcting of work set. I had a job to keep pace with him as he worked out every example and question in the books I provided. He became really good so that when the big day arrived special arrangements were made for him to sit the examination. A quick glance at his finished script showed us that he must have passed. The papers were sent off for marking and he gained very high marks. Delighted, I said to him, "Well, with this sort of result for all your work, what will you do with it?" "Change my style from nicking bluey (lead) in the East of London and move over to the West End to concentrate on sparklers (gems)." All my labour in vain — but then you can't win 'em all. If you enter the prison service with a total reforming instinct then you're doomed before you start.

How about Andy? He was a little man and (we were told) a devout Roman Catholic. He told me one evening that he had squared it right with Father Regan so that he had nothing to worry about inside. However, to put things right with God he wanted to make a confessional box! Would I show him how to make one — and me a Freechurch man! I seized the chance to go with him to the RC room where he could show me what he had in mind. I told him that I was very surprised that such a devout man was doing time, and he "opened up." "You see," he said, "it was all a mistake." (All too many say that — they were caught). "I got nicked for stealing a car but what really happened was this. For ages I've not liked people who have posh cars and don't clean 'em. Overlooking a car park off Holborn I had a room, and every day I watched City gents drive in and find their patch. They would take out their bowler and brief case, lock the car, and go off to the office — leaving the car FILTHY DIRTY. People like that shouldn't have smart cars! When they had been gone for half an hour (just in case they forgot something and came back for it) I went down, polished the car and made it look real good, then took it out for a short spin — only round the block — then took it back so that when the bloke came back I could watch his face at the sight of his car all nice and clean." "But surely," I said, "You could have asked the owner first." "Oh no, that wouldn't be the same; just to see his face was enough, I didn't want any money for doing it. I've done dozens like that." He was (to use the inside term) a "nutter" and he had only a few weeks to serve before his release. What to do with a case like this? There was only one thing to do. Let him clean the Governor's car — it needed it. He completed the little box for his RC corner, and in due course returned to — car spotting?? I don't know, but if you ever park somewhere near Holborn make sure that your car is not dirty.

My work at the prison was confined to evening teaching, and I took up a daytime appointment at Brockhill Boys School near Hythe. Brockhill is in the heart of the country and very much geared to the rural scene. I was there for just over a year and took on what was called by the Head the Remove Form. Remove meant that the boys had been a bit of a problem, to put it mildly. We had a large school farm with never less than sixty pigs and upwards of one hundred chickens. In addition, the eighty apple trees in the orchard and the half acre patch of strawberries provided all that one could ever wish for. I had a feeling that at the interview my prison experience had some influence in my being appointed. The Head said that I was to have a fairly free hand with my Remove.

Mathematics to so many young people is not the subject which "sends" them and it certainly had no appeal to my boys. However they helped me weigh up animal food in stones and quarters, and mix a 5% solution of coal tar for the winter wash for the fruit trees. All this we did on the farm under the watchful eye of our resident stockman, Tom Arnold, and other members of the staff who so often I thought were ready to get me out of trouble if necessary. When you have settled an international situation like the one I mentioned earlier in this work it takes a lot more than a few boys to niggle you, and by the way the nick helped too. The boys became quite good at weights and measures, and one of them said to me, "Sir, do you know what — you have been conning us. We won't have to do maths indoors any more, will we?" If a young teacher is reading this, take note that the way to a boy's head is often via the cowshed! Relate your subject matter to the imagination of the pupil, unless of course you teach the brainboxes — then you will need no help from me.

Brockhill was a wonderful school which had its traditions in the country and was proud of it. Perhaps it was the nearby influence of Saltwood Castle. Whatever it was I enjoyed my stay there. I must confess that I prefer the single sex school for teaching. Thank goodness our nick was not mixed.

As a carpenter, for many years before, I worked in London and I felt a "yen" to move in to that area as a teacher. Edith and I discussed it at length. She was not too keen but, wonderful wife that she is, she would not present any difficulties. There would be more job opportunities for our family which was growing up. I'll tell you more about our move in the next chapter.

Chapter 8

As a family our church played an important part in our lives. The war had left so many broken pieces around that even to get back to the damaged building was to prove quite a problem. At High Street Congregational Church several of us who had returned in one piece from the four corners of the world and the seven seas found ourselves elected to the diaconate; the week by week pulpit supply needed to be considered, so lay-preaching work took up some time in preparation and study. Edith and I had our two children, Martin and Yvonne, and now to the family circle were added two girls. These had been orphaned by the death of cousins Ena and Jim, so we took them into the family to make it complete. We were the legal guardians of Barbara and Rosemary, and never has any family been more close. Some say that blood is thicker than water; all I know is that blood makes a lot more mess. In the future our four were to learn to stand on their own feet, and the work situation in the South was something to consider.

From 1954 I felt a growing pull towards the church; much of my activity was a ministry shared by Edith in caring and sharing. Often there was not too much to share. I discussed the question of taking the examination of the Congregational Church for ministers with the Rev. Rex Coombes, and after interviews and trial sermons I was launched on a course of study which, through to ordination, lasted twenty five years — you see, I was a slow reader! In any case why should work for the ministry be crammed into a short space of time? We never know it all, and I find that although I "knew it all" when I was twenty, at sixty five I still don't know all the answers.

As a family we had formed a club for handicapped children in the area. The full story of our club work is told in another work in great detail, so here reference to it will be brief. It was this work (voluntary) which resulted in our move to the then New Town of Harlow in Essex. A TV programme mentioned that in this new town the birth rate was three times the national average. This meant that there would be three times the number of handicapped children born. THIS WAS IT — WE HAD TO MOVE TO HARLOW. In a very short time, scanning through the Times Educational Supplement, I found notice of a vacancy at Brays Grove Bi-Lateral School for a teacher in the Science Department to specialise in Rural Science. I was appointed in due course and plunged into the new town creation. Everything was new; buildings, roads, churches and pubs. There were people mainly from London and some, like us, who came from further afield. In the first year I was given the first wardenship of the Youth Centre, which meant at least two evenings at the school dealing with quite a different teenage situation. The Boys from Ilford came over one night "to do me over." They didn't — they retreated!

Mr Sid Bottoms was the Head of the School. A devout Baptist, disciplinarian and scholar. I often thought that he would have made a good CO in the Royal Engineers. Major Miller and Mr Bottoms would have got on well. They had much in common; compassion and concern about other folk, without being "sloppy" about it.

We had all moved to Harlow having in mind the work with handicapped young people, and in between building our bungalow, named WEEDIDIT, and a full timetable, the family worked out the future. Looking back, I wish that there had been a ten-day week. Edith and I transferred our church membership from Dover to the David Livingstone Congregational Church in Harlow. It had not even been built, and the folk met in a schoolroom. The building came later and so one found more interest in

Edith — the background in Jos's life

the building up of a town, which has since become the mainspring of our life. The old days of carpentry at Jesse Morgans seemed far away, but how many chips on the floor did they provide!

After a year of preparation the David Livingstone Club for Handicapped Young People became a fact. The church gave every encouragement in making available the whole premises, and some of the members assisted in the work by accounting and committee service. To put such a club on the Harlow map we invited prominent local persons, representing the Police, Health Service and the Press, to serve on an advisory council. They would point the way forward, and because of their own associations many donations came our way. It was when the town thought that the church was a subsidiary of the club that I realised one of us should move. It was us, and the next task was to find suitable premises in the town. Through the efforts of Mr Harold Larter, our Patron, we had accumulated over a thousand pounds, and also our own minibus used to collect the members and take them home after a club evening. When our present HQ site was discovered, the Harlow Urban District Council made us an interest free load of £6,000 repayable over fifteen years. The Development Corporation gave us money for equipment and many local organisations piled in with cash and voluntary labour. We moved to our new home and christened it Livingstone House. Richard Baker, OBE opened it and once again we were off to new adventures in the service of the handicapped. That was in 1965 and by 1967 the need for expansion became evident. A spot on the BBC This Week's Cause produced over two thousand pounds and enabled us to settle down to the next stage in our long term development. Still, our children of 1959 were growing up and it became obvious that one day we should just have to build our own hostel. None of the work would have been possible without the help given by the team, because the club had grown beyond all expectations. We were a fully blown youth centre for the handicapped run entirely by volunteers, and we paid our way with calling on the public for funds.

I became involved in counselling and often visitations were well outside of Harlow and correspondence worldwide. It has been our policy to serve where there is a need and this will continue, especially now that we have a society in co-trusteeship that has exactly the same motivation — THE SHAFTESBURY SOCIETY. Our hostel was opened in 1974 after much hard work by many folk who care. (Read about it in another book which was prepared for publication in the Year of the Disabled.)

Throughout all this time my studies for the ministry continued, and indeed were helped by one's involvement with people. My full time teaching post was at Netteswell Comprehensive School and after many years the work for the less able found a special name — Remedial. I don't like the name; it sounds a bit too clinical. Some places call it Compensatory Education, which is worse. Why give it a special name? Just let the children, who may have certain difficulties, go to a tutorial room. I have met some children who although good at mathematics cannot spell or even write. To some minds the word remedial carries the mark of sub-standard.

For two years I served in the County Council Adult Training Centre at Chelmsford as Manager. This was to gain experience in a full time capacity with the mentally handicapped, many of whom were members of our club in Harlow. It was interesting to see them in a work situation doing industrial work that nobody else wanted to do. If they worked hard they could earn up to £4 per week; it's not a typing error — four pounds a week. I introduced a 50/50 work/education programme which tended to cut down production and give the trainees a chance to grapple with words and numbers. One firm said that they were desperate for our output, so fresh rates were negotiated and the "workforce" had a little more on payday. How easy it is to confer about "wages" for the handicapped when you are sitting on a safe number. If the Unions really want to take up a case then they should show interest in the question of the handicapped and their problems. I gave an address to a trades council five years ago and they said that they would be looking into the question of outworkers' rates of pay generally. It must be a long look 'cause I'm still waiting to hear of the result.

Having experience in the field of technical education I knew that some of my mentally handicapped trainees were in certain skills brighter than students whom earlier I taught as normal people — that is, if you can tell me what is meant by "normal" — and it puzzled me why they did not attend part time day release classes in further education as did apprentices in the trades. I wrote to every authority in the county and received only one truly positive reply; Mr Abrams, the FE adviser for Essex, just down the road at County Hall. He arranged a special conference at which we thrashed out the subject well and truly, and fifteen of my trainees commenced studies. They still attend and by reports I receive they do well. Why not? If you go to prison you have education and if you are younger, and it's Borstal that takes you in hand, then again it's eduction for you. I believe that many other Counties have copied the pattern set by Essex. A good deal of common sense must be exercised in the interests of the handicapped, so perhaps I can sum it up with the thought, don't expect too much too soon.

One morning the local Vicar of the parish church called to see me and asked me to preach at one Sunday service; the theme was to be "The Handicapped". What an opportunity this proved to be! An Anglican pulpit for a Freechurchman. With all sorts of out-pourings I did mention in my address that if our Lord came into Chelmsford on a tour He would first learn to operate a bull dozer and then go round to churches of every denomination and say, "Give me one good reason why I

107

should not flatten the place and build on the ground homes for the aged, centres for the handicapped and dwellings for the homeless." I thought that this almost revolutionary tone would herald "my lot." On the contrary the Vicar said that this was something he would love to have said, but...... Now you know why I am a Congregationalist. We must appreciate that it is us whom God uses, and if there was ever a gentle revolutionary, He was. There's not much sense in running around with a clenched fist held in the air or a misspelt slogan poorly written on a piece of plywood — GET OUT AND DO SOMETHING USEFUL — sweat blood, if necessary. Clem Atlee was a fine example of the idea, George Lansbury another. Lord Shaftesbury, Elizabeth Fry, John Howard and a host of others, were all of them Christians.

It was from Netteswell Comprehensive School that I retired from teaching, and I like to believe that when the annals of the school are written up they will say that there was a teacher there once who loved his job in caring for the less able pupil. We had the usual farewell party, complete with cake and tiddly and in no time at all I was on my way to retirement. RETIREMENT? What do they mean? Perhaps it is the time when you can do what you want to do any time you feel like it, and the time when your life is not controlled by a bell ringing at forty-minute intervals followed by a teeming mass of young people going from mathematics to history.

Ever since our arrival in Harlow and joining the Congregational Church, I had had a busy time with preaching engagements in many parts of Essex; studies for the ministry were kept going; and in 1970 there was involvement in the discussions which preceded the union of the Presbyterian and Congregational Churches, to form what has now become the United Reformed Church. Certain churches did not elect to be part of this union, which instead of making one large denomination out of two resulted in there being three and possibly four. I did apply for recognition as a local pastor in the URC, but the powers that be decided not to agree. They had rules and regulations and I was not up to their standard. Not to worry — seven years later and a lot more reading, I was ordained into the ministry of Christ via the Congregational Federation examination, requirements established years before the formation of the URC.

On leaving Netteswell School my life became very much geared to the work of the club (a caring ministry), the church and the Royal British Legion, which made me their honourary padre. Edith and I looked for a Congregational church, this being the tradition which enabled us to put ourselves in and get out the spiritual support we needed. We visited several and finally settled to join Hadham Cross Congregational Church in 1977. The minister, the Rev. Lionel Jupp, welcomed us and somehow found out that I had been a lay preacher for many years and invited me to take a service. Soon after that he told us that his health was not good and asked if I could take a service at very short notice if the need arose. Nothing could be shorter than the notice I had (about half a minute) on the occasion at Chester many years before. There were three weekends when he phoned through his SOS, and eventually he had a stroke in the vestry just before the morning service. This was it. For the second time in my life it was "Put your skates on Smith, and take over." It's not always what we want but what God has sorted out for us, and when that happens you don't have any choice if you care about His work. I took Lionel home while a student who was in the congregation took the first half of the service. Back to the church to give the sermon, and what better text was there than: "Here am I, Lord — send me?" From September of that year I was able to visit Lionel every day until he died in February 1978. We became very close in the early days of his illness — perhaps it was because he was one of the boys who came ashore at Dunkirk — how he concealed the recurring pain he had from being shot in the arm as he made his way to a boat. How noble it was of the Germans who shot up a beaten army — but let's not harbour bitterness, although it's not easy. "And in the morning we will remember them." Lionel and I talked together about many aspects of theology and doctrine. He was the learned one and from him I discovered the importance of the sure foundation of a parson's life — humility — because so much starts at this point. It was hardly a philosophical part of our many discourses, but let me tell you of one of his comments on the day before he died. "Jos," he said wearily, "You are no better looking than on the day I first met you, and ..... see that my ministry goes on."

I was able to help at church carrying on with Lionel's timetable. This meant taking the service on Sunday, visiting the elderly and the sick, and occupying the chair at the church meetings — the central point of a good church. Just in case you don't know, in a Cong' church it is the members that decide, as they feel led, on the affairs of the church. By the way, in our little church for four years there has never been a division on any proposition made, and that is not because folk in the country are easy to sway. Our country has only been as great as its rural heritage of people and place. Although we live in the new town we must have one foot in the meadows to preserve sanity.

One evening after our church meeting I sensed that the members rather wanted me to go home quickly — they had something they wanted to sort out without my being there, so I made my way to the car park opposite. Getting into my car I heard Andrew say, "He's gone," and then he went back inside the church. The next morning there was a letter in my box from the church in which they said they had unanimously invited me to be their lay pastor. Shortly afterwards I found myself duly inducted. In just over another year, following the finalising of examination requirements, I was ordained. Now an ordination is very

110

special. One hopes that the recognition will be across the wide denominational board, so I ventured to approach the Rev. Michael McAdam, the Rector of St Andrews, in the village. Without hesitation he agreed and took what is often deemed to be the mainspring of the service — the ordination prayer. For me, as a Freechurchman, this meant so much. After all, I did start off many years ago in the Anglican Church and from Whom in addition to One Who called me could give the accolade. I once read of a man who was ordained at seventy years of age, so at sixty five it makes me still a "boy." Much has been written by the secular minded about the divisions in the Christian church. Of course, there are different traditions and organisations — why not? There is one thing that is vitally important and on it both Michael and I are in agreement. Christians are UNITED IN CHRIST. Uniformity is something we do not want, nor do we feel that our Creator would have it that way. If the Divine Deity had wanted uniformity then all people would have been coloured, all speak the same language, all roses would have been red and all the Apostles tax gatherers. I hope that I've made this clear, if not, come out to Hadham Cross one Sunday and I'll explain it all.

Much of the life of the writer has been tied up with folk who through no fault of theirs have found themselves at disadvantage — the handicapped. Since 1965, when the Harlow Urban District Council made the wonderful loan, we had been able — due to the generosity of hundreds of well wishers and the efforts of the David Livingstone Kiosks Limited (our main source of regular income) — to pay off the loan, and on May 10, 1980, at a special dinner we handed over with great pride the last payment of £500. It was a great evening, with our President, Richard Baker and his wife Margaret, together with as many of the helpers as we could seat in the hall at Epping. From the early days in the church, and very very little money, we now had property worth £150,000, and had become a

Richard Baker, at the David Livingstone Club of which he is President

registered charity, and a voluntary organisation in which within the club NOBODY is paid.

The writer can only very humbly thank all who made this dream of long ago become a fact. Someone somewhere must have had a regard for the work done by the team because in November 1980 I received a letter from the Prime Minister.

10 DOWNING STREET

From the Principal Private Secretary

IN CONFIDENCE   14 November 1980

Sir,

    The Prime Minister has asked me to inform you, in strict confidence, that she has it in mind, on the occasion of the forthcoming list of New Year Honours, to submit your name to The Queen with a recommendation that Her Majesty may be graciously pleased to approve that you be appointed a Member of the Order of the British Empire.

    Before doing so, the Prime Minister would be glad to be assured that this would be agreeable to you. I should be grateful if you would let me know by completing the enclosed form and sending it to me by return of post.

                  I am, Sir,

                      Your obedient Servant,

J J Smith Esq

Chapter 9

Buckingham Palace

The letter stated that the Prime Minister had it in mind to submit my name to Her Majesty the Queen for the award of MBE. When I saw the envelope I wondered if they wanted a club started somewhere up in Downing Street, W1. However, after a few weeks when the New Year Honours List was published — there it was — David Livingstone Club, Harlow. JJ knew then that here was the reward for having the privilege of leading a team in making the handicapped feel wanted, after all that is what most of them want — just to feel wanted. By nine o'clock the press came armed with cameras, and the phone started ringing with one caller after another. Telegrams, and the next day letters and cards. It was all a bit overwhelming. I had then to think about the great day which would inevitably come. Up to London to see the Queen. What does one wear on such an occasion? It surely would not be good enough to wear my old sports jacket, so I phoned Richard Baker, and he said that he was quite sure that Her Majesty would not mind what I wore — just like him to say that! I took other advice and it was put to me that as the medal was in many ways brought about by our handicapped youngsters, then they ought to have the pleasure of seeing the "ole man" dressed up in top hat and tails. Next stop: Moss Brothers, from whom all the gear can be hired, and what is more they will have it all correct according to the rules. Almost like being back in the army again, but not to worry. For our work to be honoured by Her Majesty in this way things had to go right.

On February 24th we made our way, Edith, Yvonne and I, to London. New coats, hats, matching handbags and new shoes (how mine pinched a bit on my wonky toe!) It was going to be a big day for my ladies as well. We were all a little bit worried as we journeyed to town and then on to the Shaftesbury Society headquarters, where they kindly made arrangements for a room at the office to be available where I could change. No way was I going up on the tube dressed in a topper! Gordon Holloway, the Society's General Secretary, kindly organised transport for us to be taken to the Palace in style. At the gates there were crowds of people all waiting expectantly. I thought for us, but had not seen the papers in which it said that an important announcement might be made from the Palace that morning. We went in after our passes and invitations had been checked at the gate, and found that the order of the day was: friends and relatives to the left and recipients to the right. Edith and Yvonne were led to a good position in the ballroom, while I together with others for medals were directed along a long corridor lined on either side by Yeomen of the Guard and Life Guards. The first impression was that with all the swords and battle axes about there was no retreat — who would want to, anyway? Eventually we were all assembled in a long room in which oil paintings of knights and dignitaries looked down at us — I thought, in approval. We were checked again and a little pin hook was fastened on our coats. Then we waited. At 10.55 precisely a gentlemen came in and called for our attention as he had an announcement to make ...... there was silence.

"I have been instructed to inform you that it is Her Majesty's wish that you know before it is officially released to the nation that Her Majesty and Prince Philip are pleased to announce the betrothal of their beloved son, Prince Charles, to Lady Diana Spencer."

Then I knew why there were crowds outside. It is not the custom to applaud at an investiture, but we all did and

I am quite sure that Her Majesty did not mind — indeed, she looked delighted.

All the recipients were divided into two groups so that in each group there were those who were to be knighted, as well as the remainder who between them were to receive the CBE, OBE and MBE, together with the various decorations awarded to the services. A further check and we were on our way to the assembly of relations and friends. Last minute instructions as to our movement just before we met the Queen, and we waited for our name and award to be announced. Slowly the recipients moved forward until we were in the ballroom. This was it — "The Reverend Josiah James Smith, MBE." I did not feel nervous. Her Majesty has the gift of putting her people at ease and her few words of encouragement made me feel very proud of the team which had made all this possible. The David Livingstone Club had received national recognition — what a wonderful day it was! Once outside the Palace the photographers moved in to take their pictures and in a short time we were once again on our way for lunch with our friends at the Shaftesbury Society headquarters.

Back to Moss Brothers to return the morning suit and topper brought my adventure to an end, although of course the work of the Club goes on, to remind me that yet another new chapter in the Club's history begins.

My folk at the church showed their delight at all the happenings of January and February, and promptly decided to add the letters MBE to the notice board. After all, over many years they added their support to the Club by their generosity and support in various ways. Bless 'em all.

The Great Day Out — 31 December 1980
Yvonne — Jos — Edith

117

Jos

Chapter 10

Or Final Clearing Up of the Chips

Not even someone famous can write beyond the description of a visit to the Palace to meet Her Majesty the Queen, so my closing words will be few.

Obviously, having reached the age when one is referred to as an OAP there are many years which one can recall. On the thesis that it is not good to dwell on the past for too long, let me look forward into the future.

We live in a changing society where standards alter almost day by day. There is always need for improvement in techniques, reasoning, design and distribution. Let us meet problems as they arise with a determination to put right those things we may have done wrongly. If the author who was pressed into writing "CHIPS ON THE FLOOR" has to pick out any one person (although there are many) it would be — indeed it is — my old foreman, Mr William Wood, who insisted that in whatever we do WE MUST DO A GOOD JOB.

I pray that this is what I have done.
That's all — so put the broom away —
And go home.